Big
Business
Economic Power in a Free Society

Big
Business
Economic Power in a Free Society

Advisory Editor
LEON STEIN

Editorial Board
.Stuart Bruchey
Thomas C. Cochran

A NOTE ABOUT THIS BOOK

A scholarly examination of company directors — their functions, training, origins, development, shortcomings, education, character, and social life. Generalizations are based on case studies of the American Tobacco Co., Climax Molybdenum Co., General Foods Corporation and Standard Oil Co. (N.J.). The *Harvard Law Review* stated that this work is "refreshing because it is an objective consideration of a rather controversial topic; informative because the facts presented are derived from first-hand contact with directors and representative industrial corporations."

DIRECTORS AND THEIR FUNCTIONS

A PRELIMINARY STUDY

JOHN CALHOUN BAKER

NYT

ARNO PRESS
A New York Times Company
New York / 1973

Reprint Edition 1973 by Arno Press Inc.

Copyright © by the President and Fellows
   of Harvard College

Reprinted by permission of The Harvard University
   Graduate School of Business Administration
Reprinted from a copy in The Newark Public Library

BIG BUSINESS: Economic Power in a Free Society
ISBN for complete set: 0-405-05070-4
See last pages of this volume for titles.

Manufactured in the United States of America

——◆——

Library of Congress Cataloging in Publication Data

Baker, John Calhoun, 1895-
   Directors and their functions.

   (Big business: economic power in a free society)
   Reprint of the 1945 ed. published by Division of
Research, Graduate School of Business Administration,
Harvard University, Boston.
   Includes bibliographical references.
   1. Directors of corporations--United States--
Case studies. I. Title. II. Series.
HD2745.B2 1973   658.4'2   73-1990
ISBN 0-405-05074-7   76-6157

DIRECTORS AND THEIR FUNCTIONS

DIRECTORS AND THEIR FUNCTIONS

A Preliminary Study

JOHN CALHOUN BAKER

President, Ohio University
Formerly Associate Dean, Harvard University, and
Professor of Business Administration, Graduate School of Business
Administration, Harvard University

Division of Research
Graduate School of Business Administration
Harvard University
Boston

1945

HARVARD UNIVERSITY

GRADUATE SCHOOL OF BUSINESS ADMINISTRATION

GEORGE F. BAKER FOUNDATION

DONALD K. DAVID, *Dean*
MELVIN T. COPELAND, *Director of Research*

Second Printing

———

Printed at The Andover Press
Andover, Massachusetts

Foreword

The directors of American business corporations carry a heavy load of responsibility. They hold key positions in the management of many of our business concerns. Their judgment and resourcefulness in selecting operating executives and their wisdom in approving administrative policies will play a major part in the job-making task which business faces in the years ahead, especially in the years immediately ahead.

Despite the key importance of directors in business management, no comprehensive, constructive study of their functions has been undertaken heretofore. Certain aspects of the duties of directors have been discussed, to be sure, in various publications, but no broad study ever has been made. The subject is one which long has interested members of the Faculty of the Harvard Business School, and in recent years an increasing number of cases on directors have been used for class discussion. Under these circumstances, members of the Faculty have especially welcomed the opportunity to undertake the research study, the first results of which are presented in this volume.

Dr. Baker's interest in this subject developed naturally out of his extensive research on the subject of executive compensation. In this first report on the study of directors, he opens up the subject and not only gives some concrete results of the research already carried on but also presents a vista of the research opportunities ahead.

The costs of this project were met from funds contributed by the Associates of the Harvard Business School.

MELVIN T. COPELAND

Director of Research

Soldiers Field
Boston, Massachusetts
June, 1945

[v]

Preface

In the last half century, American corporations have assumed a position of rapidly increasing importance in our economic, social, and political life. They have often been violently attacked and defended. Certain groups have argued that they were a great blessing to mankind and others that they were impersonal, inhuman, legal machines that were destroying individuals and society. The legal characteristics, the growth, success, failure, and many other phases of corporate activity have been studied, explained, and criticized. All too little attention, however, has been paid to corporation directors, although they are legally responsible for management. They, like executives, are faced with the problem of knowing and meeting their responsibilities and of keeping abreast of rapidly changing conditions. This book is an examination of directors and their functioning in the early 1940's based on a broad study of the directors in many corporations as well as specific policies relating to directors in four well-known American corporations.

A decade ago it probably would have been impossible to make an examination of directors such as is now undertaken. Not only are more adequate records available than existed in past years, but the attitude of directors toward their responsibilities has changed; and almost without exception full cooperation was secured from directors in all companies approached. Not only were they willing to express their opinions, but they made available records of directors' meetings and special reports and answered all questions pertaining to the subject. Without such cooperation from many different individuals this book could not have been written. A large number of directors of important corporations made clear their sincere desire to know more about their function as directors. These men were eager to know what their duties were as fiduciaries and were concerned with their responsibilities. They sought to understand the variety of interests to whom socially, if not legally, they owed an allegiance in the exercise of the "rule-making" powers. Issues of this character were found to be uppermost in the minds and inquiries of substantially all the scores of directors with whom interviews and often repeated interviews were held.

Directors, corporation executives, and corporation records furnished the basic data for this analysis. There was frequent recourse to government records and documents as well as numerous interviews with members of government commissions, executives of labor organizations, small and large stockholders, and executives who were not directors. Emphasis was placed on securing firsthand information on directors in action, their achievements and records, as well as secondary material ·uch as criticisms and legal cases. One main objective was to understand the substance of how directors functioned rather than simply the form or what the record appeared to be.

Various members of the Securities and Exchange Commission and staff were interviewed, and pertinent records of the commission examined. It should be recognized that over the last decade this commission's influence on directors has been great. Directly and indirectly laws as well as administrative rulings have turned the thoughts of both the public and directors to the latters' corporate duties and responsibilities. The perspective of history may well indicate that important, constructive results were secured in this way from laws and rulings which were attacked as being radical and destructive at the time they were made.

Broad studies of directors were undertaken to provide data on the whole subject of directors and their functions. Questions were investigated ranging all the way from "Who should be directors?" and "Should they have tenure or rotate?" to "Should directors be paid?" and "How far should they enter into the administration of their specific corporations?" This publication is only part of a more extensive research study of corporation directors which the author has been conducting for two years and which grows out of a prolonged study of executive functions and compensation. (*Executive Salaries and Bonus Plans*, 1938). Certain other important aspects of the problem that are being studied further are the legal, political, social, and economic environment in which directors must function; the motivation, remuneration, source, selection, and retirement of directors; the use of executive, financial, and advisory committees; analysis of proposed panaceas, such as representation of the public, labor, or consumers on boards of directors; and the ethics or philosophy of directors in relation to American life. These merely indicate certain additional important phases of the whole subject of directors. The role of management, including both directors and executives, in modern life calls for much further study.

It also should be pointed out that most of the directorates studied were those of medium-size and large companies classified as industrial. There was scattered examination of the directors in railroads, public utilities, banks, and insurance companies, but the conclusions in this book have been little influenced by those incidental studies and it should not be inferred that the findings would necessarily apply to any other group than listed American industrial corporations.

It is important to recognize that so far as directors are concerned, there are important differences between publicly owned and privately owned companies. The companies analyzed in this project are publicly owned in the sense that General Motors Corporation is—with its stock listed and with thousands of stockholders. In contrast, the stock of the Ford Motor Company is unlisted and privately owned by a few stockholders.

Because of the excellent cooperation of the executives and directors in many companies, frequent reference is made to the policies of specific corporations. Special acknowledgment is due to the officers and directors of The American Tobacco Company, Climax Molybdenum Company, General Foods Corporation, and Standard Oil Company (New Jersey) for their willingness to make available the material used in preparation of the detailed studies of directors' policies in their specific companies. Each company had a distinct tradition and corporate personality. The companies varied widely in directorates, problems faced, products, size, age, and management. *All, however, were profitable, even though the policies and practices of their directorates varied widely.* These companies were not selected to feature them in any way or to expose their policies to criticism. The executives and directors of these companies furnished the information required. They did not concern themselves with, nor have they any responsibility for, my choice of data, comparisons, findings, and conclusions.

The four cases indicate something of each company's individuality by references to its history, products, organization, informal human relations and traditions, methods of communication between executives and directors, directors' meetings and minutes, and problems considered, as background for brief outlines of directors in action. Obviously, within the space available, we have been able to give only a thumbnail sketch of each company.

A committee composed of Professors Ralph J. Baker, George E. Bates, Melvin T. Copeland, and myself originally planned this study. All members of the committee had in past years been interested in directors and their functioning. Professor Ralph Baker had given this subject especial attention as a member of the Harvard Law School Faculty. Professor Bates wrote a pioneer article ("The Board of Directors," *Harvard Business Review*, Autumn, 1940) on the subject, and he and Professor Copeland have discussed some of these problems in their course in Administrative Policy in the Harvard Business School.

All the members of the group took an active part in the initial conferences with numerous directors and executives, but their subsequent participation in the study was interfered with by wartime teaching and administrative duties. The responsibility for carrying on this specific study was therefore delegated to me. The assistance which I received from this group, and specifically from Professor Melvin T. Copeland, I appreciate deeply. For the arrangement of this book and its findings and interpretations I am solely responsible and must accept all criticism.

Mr. Andrew R. Towl has assisted me at many stages of the study, from personal interviews to the final draft of the manuscript. He and Miss Marian V. Sears have borne the detailed labor of preparing specific cases and getting much of the material in shape for publishing. Their criticisms and suggestions have been invaluable, and to both of them I am deeply grateful. This bare acknowledgment in no way cancels my debt to them. Finally, I want to express my appreciation for the assistance of many businessmen, my colleagues, and others, with whom I have frequently discussed the problems of corporation directors and from whom I have received constructive ideas and criticisms. Without the help of all these individuals to whom acknowledgment is made, this study could never have been completed.

JOHN CALHOUN BAKER

Athens, Ohio
June, 1945

TABLE OF CONTENTS

CHAPTER I

Directors and Their Environment

THE course of public interest in social and economic problems generally follows a well-defined pattern. This is true of the current concern over corporation directors. Here as in other similar problems the symptoms of a condition, with almost violent interest on the part of a small minority, appear first. This is followed by a period of substantial activity accompanied by wide public discussion. The concluding period is one with solutions or partial solutions followed by a decline of public interest. The issues may then be forgotten, unless the solution creates numerous acute abuses. Interest in the problems surrounding corporation directors has followed this typical pattern and in 1945 is passing from its first to its second phase. These facts alone justify a serious analysis of the problems in this area. During such periods all knowledge possible should be available, particularly to the public, which is the final judge on questions of broad social significance.

Directors, executives, stockholders, students of government, and others have asked many questions about directors and their environment which on the surface seem to be unrelated but which fundamentally are so interdependent that no ready answer can be given to any one: for example, Who are directors? What are their responsibilities? Do directors control corporations? Should a company have all "inside" (executive) directors or should it have in addition certain "outside" (nonexecutive) directors? Is profit an adequate measure of corporate success? Should directors be paid substantial annual salaries or simply the traditional fees? Should retirement plans be developed and enforced for directors? What makes directors good directors? Should various groups such as labor, small stockholders, customers, and others have representatives on directorates? Should there be a geographical and industrial distribution of directors on a board? Should directors have what amounts to tenure or should they rotate? Should a company favor a policy of permitting its officers to be directors in other companies? How do the functions of directors vary from those of corporate executives? Answers to these and similar questions are important to directors so that they may know how to meet their duties properly and just as important to stockholders and the public so that they may have a basis on which to judge directors and their contributions in a democratic society.

No attempt will be made in this book to answer all these questions, but these and many more must be answered before the role of the director can be completely defined.

Three aspects of the complex background suggested by these questions, however, need to be mentioned even though adequate treatment is beyond the scope of this book: the separation of ownership from management, the growing social significance of corporations, and the emerging concept of trusteeship.

The separation of ownership from management in business corporations is of particular significance to the role of directors. In early corporate history most companies were small, and directors, executives, and stockholders were one group; often one individual was in all three positions. Slowly stockholdings became distributed, and companies grew in size and issued more stock. No longer were stockholders and directors identical. Stockholders elected directors to represent them and lost interest in details of operations. They were concerned mainly with success as expressed in terms of earnings, dividends, and stock values; executives operated the companies. This pattern of corporate evolution may be repeated in broad outline by each successful, growing corporation. The problems arising from this condition have long been looked at with concern, as the following quotation from a document written in 1863 indicates:

> Time has changed the relations of owners and managers, until only traces of their original condition remain. The originators — large stockholders, or principal owners, as they were called — of these institutions have died (three or four

only of them are now left, and they are feeble old men); their estates have been distributed to their heirs, and sold out to the public.... The present stockholders...rarely know each other at all. They are scattered all over New England, and even other States. They have bought their shares as an investment, and with the delusive hope that somebody is interested in it who can and will take care of it.[1]

Nevertheless, separation of ownership from management has continued. As the trend developed, key executives or a small controlling group, rather than stockholders as a whole, selected and induced individuals to serve as directors.[2] The number of stockholders, particularly small stockholders, in many publicly owned concerns, has increased rapidly in the last fifteen years. Stockholders in Procter & Gamble Company, for instance, numbered about 13,000 in 1929, and by 1944 had increased to nearly 45,000. The position of a stockholder, furthermore, has become less like that of an owner or an entrepreneur and more like that of an investor. Close cooperation between stockholders and directors has been difficult and often nonexistent. The responsibilities of both directors and executives as well as the line between them have been hazy and have varied from company to company.

The increasing social significance of corporations is another factor to be emphasized in the complex background in which directors function. The "New Deal" of the 1930's formalized in laws and administrative rulings[3] many trends that were emerging in the "New Era" of the late 1920's. Full disclosure

[1]James Cook Ayer, *Some of the Usages and Abuses in the Management of Our Manufacturing Corporations* (Lowell, Massachusetts, C. M. Langley & Co., 1863), p. 3.

[2]Examples of exceptions follow:
One company's experience is recounted in the pamphlet *Report of the Stockholders Investigating Committee of The Texas Corporation*, January 25, 1934.
In 1929, in protest against the part of the chairman of Standard Oil Company of Indiana in a Senate investigation, Mr. John D. Rockefeller, Jr., sought to prevent his reelection to the board. Mr. Rockefeller actively solicited proxies from other minority stockholders and against considerable opposition by a group supporting the chairman succeeded in controlling a majority of the votes cast at the annual meeting in March.

[3]The Securities and Exchange Commission, for instance, is concerned with directors in its administration of the following seven laws: Securities Act of 1933, Securities Exchange Act of 1934, Public Utility Holding Company Act of 1935, Trust Indenture Act of 1939, Investment Company Act of 1940, Investment Advisers Act of 1940, and Bankruptcy Act, Ch. X. See *The Work of the Securities and Exchange Commission* (Washington, Government Printing Office, 1944).

of operating results as well as widespread publicity[1] have become accepted practice in corporate affairs. It is now rare for a large corporation to follow the policy of "no or low visability." Stockholders, as well as the public in general, are showing increased interest in corporate problems and directors. That there has been considerable justification for much latent as well as expressed misunderstanding and dissatisfaction cannot be doubted. Stockholders, particularly small ones, in the past have frequently been ignored and occasionally "frozen out" of what many considered to be their rights. In the opinion of certain directors, officers, and others, small stockholders, or any stockholders for that matter, have been necessary nuisances and could "sell their stock if they did not like the way a company was managed." This answer is both too simple and unfair. Furthermore, it accepts as desirable a rapid turnover of small stockholders, neglects a consideration of the social and political implications inherent in our large corporations, and overlooks the political and other support which management may derive from this rapidly increasing group of individuals. Special organizations of stockholders, recognizing the importance of corporations and difficulty of individual effort with diffused ownership, are attempting to concentrate the support of widely scattered owners into associations and thus make their cooperative power effective.[2] Individual stockholders are making widespread use of a provision

[1]An experiment to keep stockholders informed of current conditions was reported by Mr. Lewis H. Brown, president of Johns-Manville Corporation, in the 1941 Annual Report to Stockholders. "More than 1,200 Johns-Manville stockholders attended twelve regional informal stockholder meetings held in as many cities in the United States during February and March, 1941. From the results of a poll taken among stockholders these meetings were favorably received and many stockholders suggested that they be continued." The policy was continued but restricted in 1943 and 1944 because of wartime conditions.

Merrill Griswold, chairman of Massachusetts Investors Trust, in a speech before the National Association of Securities Commissioners in Cincinnati in September, 1943, urged investment trusts to consider themselves the representatives of the small shareholder. He warned against interpreting "stockholder quiescence as acquiescence."

[2]At a clinic on management compensation held under the auspices of the Investors Fairplay League in January, 1945, Congressman Ellsworth B. Buck made the following statement: "It is my firm conviction that investors can gain a place in the sun, and exert their fair influence on the course of local, state and national legislation, if they will borrow a page from the book of the times and form organizations to represent them competently." *Bulletin*, Investors Fairplay League, February, 1945, p. 2.

in the regulations of the Securities and Exchange Commission that security holders may have proposals, together with a 100-word supporting statement, included in the management's proxy soliciting material. For instance, the Proxy Statement of the P. Lorillard Company dated February 5, 1943, contained the following items presented by the holder of ten shares of the common stock.

RESOLUTION NUMBER 2.

Resolved that the present Board of Directors, which is responsible for recommendation of men to serve on the succeeding Board of Directors, shall nominate for the coming fiscal period at least six men who are *not* a part of the present management, and who are not connected with the management of any of the P. Lorillard Company subsidiaries.

Reason for Resolution Number 2.

It is important that in the selection of management and in the formation of policy, the Board of Directors should be free of any management [executive] domination. Otherwise, management would tend to perpetuate itself and the directors would fail to be representatives of the common stockholders who are the owners of the company. They need the advantage of members on the Board who can bring outside viewpoint and a variety of business experience.

The separation of ownership from management and the social aspects of corporations direct attention to the emerging concept of trusteeship. This growing concern about the concept of trusteeship also arises from the vaguely defined position of trustees in eleemosynary corporations and other institutions. One member of a board of trustees stated the situation as follows: "The delegation of the powers of the state to the trustees is so free and dimly defined, especially in matters of nonfinancial policies, that the trustees' responsibility is proportionately increased." In this study, *trusteeship* is used in a popular sense to describe this attitude of directors toward their position, and this usage has no reference to title to property or other legal implications. There is no intention of engaging in the practical and theoretical problems of transferring precedents from the law of trusts to the consideration of corporation

[5]

directors.[1] Our concern is with the keen sense of broad responsibility that most directors evidenced as they confronted the growing number of small stockholders and the great social obligations of large corporations. Mr. Owen D. Young, then chairman of the board, General Electric Company, summarized this point of view in an address, "What Is Right in Business?" in January, 1929.

> ...Very soon he saw rising a notion that managers were no longer attorneys for stockholders; they were becoming trustees of an institution.
> ...If I am a trustee, who are the beneficiaries of the trust? To whom do I owe my obligations?
> My conception of it is this: That there are three groups of people who have an interest in that institution. One is the group of fifty-odd thousand people who have put their capital in the company, namely, its stockholders. Another is a group of well toward one hundred thousand people who are putting their labor and their lives into the business of the company. The third group is of customers and the general public.
>
> * * * * *
>
> I think what is right in business is influenced very largely by the growing sense of trusteeship which I have described. One no longer feels the obligation to take from labor for the benefit of capital, nor to take from the public for the benefit of both, but rather to administer wisely and fairly in the interest of all.

There have been many partial studies of the complex background of corporations in which the separation of ownership from management, the growing social significance of corporations, and the emerging concept of trusteeship are but three elements. It is difficult, however, to define any single factor in this problem apart from the others. It is necessary to understand the interaction of all factors. For instance, the historic study of *The Modern Corporation and Private Property* made by Adolf A. Berle, Jr., and Gardiner C. Means in 1933 was followed by many other studies of the general phenomena. Such studies throw important light on the subject. Most studies

[1] See, for instance, E. Merrick Dodd, Jr., "For Whom Are Corporate Managers Trustees?" *Harvard Law Review*, May, 1932, p. 1145. Also Adolf A. Berle, Jr., "For Whom Corporate Managers *Are* Trustees: A Note," *Harvard Law Review*, June, 1932, p. 1365.

that begin from the general point of view, however, usually fall short of carrying through their analysis to an understanding of management in individual enterprises. On the other hand, writers on business organization have too frequently terminated their analyses of management functions by perfunctorily placing a box for the board of directors at the top of an organization chart. Likewise legal treatises have been limited in their attempts to interpret the statutes creating and regulating corporations and the court opinions arising from decisions of specific cases.[1]

A difficulty common to all studies made in this field, including the present one, is that of keeping all factors in proper perspective. The full role of the director is revealed not only by a study of what he does in specific companies and how he func-

---

[1]Although not a complete bibliography, the following works are stimulating illustrations of different points of view:

Howard H. Spellman, *A Treatise on the Principles of Law Governing Corporate Directors* (New York, Prentice-Hall, Inc., 1931).

Adolf A. Berle, Jr., and Gardiner C. Means, *The Modern Corporation and Private Property* (New York, The MacMillan Company, 1933).

Adolf A. Berle, Jr., and Victoria J. Pederson, *Liquid Claims and National Wealth*, An Exploratory Study in the Theory of Liquidity (New York, The MacMillan Company, 1934).

Luther H. Gulick and L. Urwick, editors, *Papers on the Science of Administration* (New York, Columbia University, Institute of Public Administration, 1937).

National Resources Committee, *The Structure of the American Economy*, Part I, Basic Characteristics (Washington, Government Printing Office, June, 1939).

U. S. Temporary National Economic Committee, *Investigation of Concentration of Economic Power*, Hearings and Monographs (Washington, Government Printing Office, 1939-1941).

George E. Bates, "The Board of Directors," *Harvard Business Review*, Autumn, 1940, p. 72.

E. Merrick Dodd, Jr., and Ralph J. Baker, *Cases on Business Associations, Corporations* (Chicago, The Foundation Press, Inc., 1940).

James Burnham, *The Managerial Revolution*, What is Happening in the World (New York, The John Day Company, Inc., 1941).

Paul E. Holden, Lounsbury S. Fish, and Hubert L. Smith, *Top-Management Organization and Control* (Stanford University, California, Stanford University Press, 1941).

John W. Scoville and Noel Sargent, compilors, *Fact and Fancy in the T.N.E.C. Monographs*, Reviews of the 43 monographs issued by the Temporary National Economic Committee (New York, Sponsored by the National Association of Manufacturers, 1942).

Peter F. Drucker, *The Future of Industrial Man, A Conservative Approach* (New York, The John Day Company, Inc., 1942).

Robert A. Brady, *Business as a System of Power* (New York, Columbia University Press, 1943).

Robert A. Gordon, *Business Leadership in the Large Corporation* (Washington, The Brookings Institution, 1945).

Beardsley Ruml, *Tomorrow's Business* (New York, Farrar & Rinehart, Inc., 1945).

tions but also by wider inquiry into what is expected of him, the results of his decisions, and what his contribution to society should be. This approach might well lead even farther afield to certain very fundamental philosophical questions, such as this: Is a free society best? No attempt will be made to answer this and similar tempting questions; the objectives of this study are limited to the functioning of.directors in our present-day, free democratic society. Even a program with such limitations is sufficiently broad. These limitations still leave with both directors and research students the large social, economic, and business problems faced by directors themselves dealing with the relationships of business to government, a healthy economy, profitable corporations, employee and labor relations, a high level of employment, opportunities for youth, relations with stockholders, and a host of other serious questions.

Directors, from the Management Viewpoint

The study, of which this book is the first result, started with management problems that large industrial corporations must meet and the relationship of directors to these management problems. Through an objective approach it was hoped to pierce traditional concepts and avoid academic abstractions. Complications, however, arose from the first, particularly when the solution to specific questions depended upon the solutions to over-all questions, such as the broad social implications of directors' functions or an adequate and acceptable philosophy of their duties. Businessmen and their legal advisers have for the most part failed to appreciate these implications fully. Changes and innovations in management are taking place, partly as a result of current economic, social, and political conditions, and partly as a result of new laws and developing concepts of businessmen, economists, lawyers, and governmental agencies. Old titles of "board chairman" or "executive committee" have new meanings. Customs and traditions are no longer sufficient to indicate a course of action; a new philosophy is required within which businessmen and their advisers may act. Such complexities indicated that this analysis should stress principles as well as techniques and practices, and that conclusions should be more constructive than simply discovery and listing of the functions of directors and reporting on whether they performed them well. All the questions as well as the entire investigation led to the heart of this analysis — the present-day contributions and responsibilities of directors in management.

Throughout the study of directors in management two streams of thought recur. One of these has to do with the part directors play in *administration*, that is, in getting things done; their administrative know-how, or the drive needed to achieve profits. The other stream of thought has to do with the part directors play in *trusteeship*, that is, in keeping a balance among the interests of stockholders, employees, customers, and the public. Another aspect of trusteeship is the part directors play in freeing executives from charges such as self-dealing in setting their own salaries.

A word of caution about trusteeship may well be added: directors must avoid the pitfalls of a narrow, protective, trust-management viewpoint in thinking of their fiduciary role. Both administrative skill and sense of trusteeship are essential to directors. Directors and executives must think in terms of securing corporate success in the broadest sense. Corporations must venture; must take business risks. For this, a larger initiative and more willingness to take reasonable risks are essential than in the management of a trust estate.

Much light can be thrown on directors and their functions by studies of pathological situations and by revealing abuses, but it is equally, if not more, important to examine the policies and practices of directors under normal conditions. This book follows the latter course, and stresses what directors in successful companies did and how they did it. Attention is given to criticisms encountered, but throughout, the emphasis is on the constructive job of directors.

One chief executive has aptly described the role of directors as follows: "Many of the abuses of the past came about through representation on the Board of special interests. We are using the word democracy today in so many confusing ways and representation of minorities is being confused with group pressures. We hear of claims in the name of democracy that labor should be represented on boards of directors and that small stockholders should be represented, and that directors should be representatives of the various interests among the stockholders. All of this overlooks the fact that the essential purpose of a board of directors is to represent the corporation as a whole and solely for the best interest of the corporation."

In conclusion, the role of directors can be adequately defined only in terms of the whole complex environment of business enterprise. This book seeks to keep in perspective the broad implications of the role of directors. At the same time the approach and the emphasis throughout are from the standpoint of business management. Specifically the objective is to throw light on the management functions of directors, the methods of performing these functions, trends in the attitudes and functions of directors, the characteristics of an able director, the need of adapting boards to the personalities and problems of individual companies, and the possibility of making boards more effective by clarifying the concept of trusteeship and the position of the board chairman. Directors appear to be at the crossroads; they need to know their duties and meet them adequately, or drastic changes may well occur which would completely revolutionize the character of the control and supervision of American business and industry.

CHAPTER II

Directors and Their Problems

THE preceding chapter describes the role of the director in terms of the whole complex environment of modern corporations, and indicates that this book analyzes the subject from the viewpoint of the directors' management functions. The first step was to interview many directors and executives of large industrial corporations. These interviews were supplemented by study of minutes, financial records, literature, and other sources. The resulting composite picture of directors and management problems gives perspective, but tends to blur interrelationships which subsequent chapters help clarify by more specific case studies.

The purpose of this chapter is to report from the broad study some of the common problems confronting directors in management, methods used, points of view, and criticisms encountered, with a brief analysis of certain suggested remedies.

At the outset it is important to recognize that corporations are created by laws which give boards of directors management responsibilities. Although this book does not attempt to analyze corporation law, some legal aspects[1] require attention. According to the General Corporation Law of the State of Delaware, which is fairly typical, the position of directors is as follows: "The business of every corporation organized under the provisions of this Chapter shall be managed by a board of Directors...."[2] Furthermore, "Corporate acts result from an 'order of the board of directors' and not from the individual

---

[1]For a survey of legal concepts and cases dealing with directors see E. Merrick Dodd, Jr., and Ralph J. Baker, *Cases on Business Associations, Corporations* (Chicago, The Foundation Press, Inc., 1940), Volume I, Ch. VI, "Directors' Duties and Remedies for Their Enforcement." See also Howard H. Spellman, *A Treatise on the Principles of Law Governing Corporate Directors* (New York, Prentice-Hall, Inc., 1931).

[2]General Corporation Law of the State of Delaware, revised to April 9, 1941, Art. 1, Ch. 65, Sec. 9.

action of the members of that board; the action of the board must be based upon the determinations of a majority present at a properly convened board meeting."[1] "Directors...can lawfully act only at meetings...a majority of the board being necessary at common law to constitute a quorum.,.. The modern rule permitting shareholders to vote by proxy is inapplicable to directors."[2] Volumes of court opinion have been written on the application of law to specific cases.

Under the system of directorates which has developed in this country among large, listed companies, directors are unable to "manage" corporations in any narrow interpretation of the word. Over the years directors have delegated, both consciously and unconsciously, most of their specific functions to executives. Directors do not and cannot "direct" corporations in the sense of operating them. Nevertheless, directors are an important part of top management.[3]

The responsibility of top management, which includes both directors and executives, is defined as the welfare of the entire enterprise. This responsibility implies more than the dovetailing and coordinating of production, marketing, finance, and administrative controls. Top management is responsible for the determination and revision of corporate purposes and objectives in accordance with social trends. It also must achieve these objectives with profit. Top management must determine sound principles, strategy, and policies, and implement them with an administrative organization plan and controls which attract and develop competent personnel.

Management Functions of Directors Vary

Management problems considered by boards varied widely from company to company in the study, but taken as a whole, they covered practically the entire range of top management functions. Some executives, it is true, maintained that the board's only function is to elect the president, and at the other

[1]Spellman, op. cit., p. 7.
[2]Dodd and Baker, op. cit., p. 261.
[3]For illustration of many discussions of the executive's role in top management, see Chester I. Barnard, *The Functions of the Executive* (Cambridge, Harvard University Press, 1938); Walter S. Gifford, "Some Thoughts on Organization and Executive Work," *Bell Telephone Magazine*, June, 1942 [1922 article reprinted], p. 80; and Holden, Fish, and Smith, op. cit., particularly pp. 1-12.

extreme, some directors gave reasons for a board's attempt to operate a company. The following incomplete compilation of statements suggests the scope and variety of problems reported.

One of the main functions of directors is to secure competent executives to operate a company and to insure the continuation of able management. As a corollary to this, directors must be ready to act as a "stand-by" for executives if they for any reason fail. Directors are particularly active in case of near failure, receivership, or similar crises.

Directors consider and approve the basic policies under which a corporation operates, such as the following: what products should be made, what facilities used, how products should be sold, and how financed; also price policies, important advertising policies, and other relations with consumers, distributors, labor, and government.

Directors check executives and the results they secure. This not only means analyzing financial results, such as sales volume, profits, competitive position, public relations, and similar problems, but also the character of executives, possibility of dishonesty or extravagance.

Directors supervise, control, and act on important financial matters, such as capital structure changes, large loans, dividend payments, and relations with subsidiaries.

Directors approve and review capital and operating budgets.

Directors approve selection of general counsel and formal action required by law.

Directors establish the salaries of senior executives, approve bonus and pension plans, and control all other policies relating to payments to executives.

Directors have the critical function of asking discerning questions at board meetings.

Directors are responsible for presenting an outside point of view. They see that proper basic relationships exist among all groups: stockholders, the public, creditors, labor, and customers.

Directors represent *all* stockholders.

Directors inspect properties and review actual operations. This furnishes them with firsthand impressions of the achievement of executives.

Directors are responsible for proper inside as well as outside audits. Some boards provide that auditors should report to outside directors and even to stockholders rather than to executives who are directors.

Directors scrutinize, or have legal counsel or expert consultants do so for them, all corporate action affecting their trustee relationships: whether the company is being legally operated; whether questionable contracts exist between officers, directors, and the corporation; whether the company is maintaining its competitive position; and similar questions.

Except for the corporate "housekeeping chores" that must be legally validated by formal board action, there seems to be little uniformity in the division of duties between directors and executives. The president of an outstanding company, who has had broad experience as a director on many different boards, concluded that directors have three functions: (1) to find and support or discharge the president, (2) to have independent ideas, and (3) to stop action on questionable projects. The chief executive of a large company concluded his discussion of directors by giving a list of problems they ought to be considering; this included public relations, selection of management, organization changes, capital expenditures, and labor relations. He, too, emphasized the importance of directors' being qualified to ask questions and check management through having a sound philosophy and concept of the management function. He defined his qualifications for directors as consisting of an understanding of what good organization ought to be, recognition of the right men for the right executive positions, skill in analyzing plans, and mastery of the technique of managing by exceptions to established policies.

Most functions at the top management level call for both administrative skill and the trusteeship point of view, with variations in emphasis. One board chairman illustrated this dual responsibility in explaining his company's decision on conversion to war production. His plant was located in a relatively small community and produced equipment with skilled workers. Two alternatives were presented to the board. The directors were satisfied after preliminary reports by executives that the organization could develop either proposal economically. The board finally decided to accept the alternative that would not require an expanded labor force, for which they could see no need in normal times. They argued that maintenance of community stability was part of their responsibility.

This choice involved a considerable understanding of administrative problems as well as a sense of trusteeship. The same board later authorized voluntary renegotiation of government contracts, a decision requiring less administrative skill but a sense of public policy.

The drive for profits in top management in most companies puts sufficient emphasis on the administrative point of view, but frequently the trusteeship obligations are not fully appreciated and are sometimes almost completely overlooked.[1] Directors should be concerned with the administrative aspects of problems and should check to see that executives secure results. Yet the board should not be preoccupied with day-to-day administrative operations. Directors need to give their attention to a large number of management duties calling for a keen sense of trusteeship which are becoming increasingly prominent: for example, deciding labor policy,[2] voting dividends, acting on stockholders' complaints, making plans for succession, checking the results of officers, and making decisions which might involve conflicts of interest. When action on these issues has been left to executive officers, it sometimes has led to public misunderstanding, mistakes, and legal controversies. This study revealed, however, that directors individually and as a group are becoming much more conscious of these fiduciary duties than ever before. Today, in almost all companies, directors are giving increased consideration to the fulfillment of these responsibilities.

[1]"I venture to assert that when the history of the financial era which has just drawn to a close comes to be written, most of its mistakes and its major faults will be ascribed to the failure to observe the fiduciary principle...." Harlan F. Stone, "The Public Influence of the Bar," *Harvard Law Review*, November, 1934, p. 8.

[2]For illustration, "...the company represents more than the 'big bosses,' New York, the stockholders, or board of directors. It is more than an economic unit with merely economic functions. The company is also an entity on which they project their greatest hopes and fears....It is the function of the policies of the company to preserve the values by means of which the social organization is maintained in a steady state of equilibrium...." Fritz J. Roethlisberger and William J. Dickson, *Management and the Worker* (Cambridge, Harvard University Press, 1939), p. 368. Also pertinent are charts of "The Informal Supervisory Organization," p. 362, and "Interrelations among Four Groups in Industry," p. 543 in Chapter XXIII, "Formal vs. Informal Organization." Also see Clinton S. Golden and Harold J. Ruttenberg, *The Dynamics of Industrial Democracy* (New York, Harper & Bros., 1942), Chapter III, "The Development of Leadership." Also Benjamin M. Selekman, "Administering the Union Agreement," *Harvard Business Review*, Spring, 1945, p. 299.

Although the composite statement of functions reported by all directors interviewed covers most top management functions, directors' methods of dealing with these problems vary widely from company to company, and even within the same company from year to year as personnel changes.

Varied Management Problems Call for Appropriate Methods of Board Action

If directors are to meet their increasing responsibilities, it seems clear that they must devote more thought to planning board activities and developing a philosophy for action. Reference has been made to the analogy between corporate and political government,[1] especially in the separation of the legislative or policy-making functions and the executive functions. Without pressing the analogy into its controversial aspects, it is pertinent in this connection to note the statement made by an experienced lawyer and successful corporation president: "I think that one of the things which should be stressed is that a board of directors is essentially a legislative body. Corporate organizations have been modeled somewhat after the American Constitution, and I think this is necessary. A Congress cannot do executive work. Executive work must peak up to a man. Once a policy is adopted, the execution of that policy must be left to the chief executive and his staff."

Study of the procedures followed by active and successful boards of directors led to the conclusion that there are at least four major variations in the way effective boards function on different questions.

One procedure has been for the board of directors to take jurisdiction of an issue, to deliberate, and to *decide*. Usually the board restricts this procedure to those areas in which it cannot delegate responsibility. Examples are the selection of a president, determining his compensation, or making a radical change in the objective of a business. In dealing with this type of problem, the board may initiate investigation; in any event, as a group it goes through the process of deliberating, determining a course of action, settling or adjudicating conflicts, and coming to a decision.

[1]See Beardsley Ruml, *Tomorrow's Business.*

[16]

A second type of board procedure relates to its action on decisions made by executives "subject to approval by the board." Illustrative of such matters are the settlement of lawsuits, selection of banks, and determination of programs. Here the board questions and checks on executive proposals. Effective directors, because they understand business administration, ask discerning questions. They probe the thoroughness with which executives diagnose problems and plan proposals. The board, after questioning, *confirms*, authenticates, and validates the executive decision; in rare cases it refuses confirmation.

Although refusal to confirm is infrequent, this fact does not reflect a rubber stamp attitude. When executives know that the board will follow the procedure of questioning their proposals, they support them with careful diagnosis and planning.

A third procedure by which board members act is in informal conferences with executives. This method is used in initial stages of policy formation. When a new line of products is under consideration or changes in executive organization are contemplated, for example, executives frequently discuss these questions with board members who *counsel*, advise, encourage, and guide executives, or give words of caution.

A fourth way that boards function is to keep abreast of executive acts by *review* of reports and inspection of facilities. By receiving reports, the board tacitly approves, or at least accepts, the acts of executives.

The way the boards in the study differed in their use of these four procedures in dealing with different questions is shown in Exhibit 1. The exhibit contains a brief list of problems selected from those found in the study. It shows the type of action taken by the boards in most companies, many companies, and in few companies. The four types of procedure are indicated by the key concept of what the boards of directors do: *decide, confirm, counsel, review*.

The meaning of Exhibit 1 is shown in the following illustration. One of the general problems listed in this exhibit is "Formation of major policies in production, marketing, finance, personnel." Consider the case of an equipment manufacturing company selling through agents. The sales manager

EXHIBIT I. METHODS USED BY DIRECTORS IN DIFFERENT COMPANIES TO DEAL WITH ILLUSTRATIVE PROBLEMS

Problems	*Methods Used by Directors*		
	In Most Companies	*In Many Companies*	*In Few Companies*
Selection of president — his remuneration (and removal)	Decide		
Nomination of directors	Decide		
Changes in capital structure	Decide		
Capital budget or expenditures	Decide	Confirm	
Selection of outside auditors	Decide	Confirm	
Determination of dividends	Decide	Confirm	
Selection and remuneration of other executives	Confirm	Decide	
Formation of postwar plans	Counsel	Confirm	Decide
Formation of major policies in production, marketing, finance, personnel	Counsel	Confirm	Decide
Addition of new products	Review	Counsel	Confirm
Preparation of operating budget	Review	Counsel	Confirm
Union negotiations and settlement	Review	Counsel	Confirm
Reports on competitive position and operating results		Review	Counsel
Decisions on detailed advertising program			Review

NOTE: This exhibit is not a statistical summary. Too few underlying data were comparable enough for mathematical count. The author believes, however, that the results are a useful approximation of the practices he and his associates observed.

proposed to the president that the company open its own sales branches. The estimated annual operating budget for the branches exceeded the usual annual capital expenditures of the entire company. Hypothetically, in most companies the president would confer with individual directors and then make his decision; in many companies the executives would develop a plan and submit it to the board for confirmation; and in a few companies the issue would be presented to the board for initial deliberation and decision. In the case cited, executives conferred with influential directors and then conducted an experiment in one area. The president reported results to the board, announcing that the executives were extending the policy nationally.

Certain boards work out with executives standards of procedure for different types of questions. They determine in general under what circumstances the directors are to decide, confirm, counsel, or merely review. Many boards still leave entirely to executives the selection of issues on which the board will act where board action is not required by law. Many directors, however, were concerned about their responsibility for care, prudence, consultation, investigation, seeking advice, and making decisions. They were perplexed concerning where they should step forward to advise and where to direct or restrain, and where they should refrain from either and leave the conduct of corporate affairs to executives. They also were considering the circumstances in which management should be supported or in which the serious step of a motion should be considered and applied.

The most effective directors, by general agreement, are those who ask the most discerning questions. The importance of this criterion is apparent when one realizes that the place of the board rightfully is removed from operations. One of the contributions a director can make to management is an independent point of view. A board can soundly decide few questions from the personal knowledge of its members. But directors can use the effective tool of asking intelligent questions to reveal blind spots in executive proposals. It seems worth while to emphasize the importance and value of the capacity of a director to ask such questions. The courts have rather strongly insisted on the principle that a corporation is ordinarily bound only by action of directors taken at a meeting. Judges apparently regard as important the opportunity for consultation. There seems to have been recognition by judges of the principle that the wiser conclusion, whether it is to act or not to act or to postpone for further investigation, is the result of consultation rather than circularization. "The foreknowledge that searching questions will be asked is a psychological barrier to the proposal of half-baked projects," to quote one forceful vice president. Furthermore, by asking questions directors do not get involved in making decisions[1] that rightly are the responsibility of executives. This procedure tends to

[1] "Not to decide questions that are not pertinent at the time is uncommon good sense, though to raise them may be uncommon perspicacity. Not to decide questions prematurely is to refuse commitment of attitude or the development of prejudice. Not to make decisions that cannot be made effective is to refrain from destroying authority. Not to make decisions that others should make is to preserve morale, to develop competence, to fix responsibility, and to preserve authority." Chester I. Barnard, *The Functions of the Executive*, p. 194.

keep directors out of operations and to help them think in terms of objectives and policies.

Criticisms Reveal Public Misunderstanding and Shifting Standards for Appraising Directors

In a field as vital as that of corporate directors it is particularly important to understand dissatisfactions and criticisms from whatever source they may come. Somewhat typical of critical comments made by businessmen interviewed was the following: "A company with which I have been working has never given proper thought to the definition of responsibilities for its Board of Directors. In fact, the Board has had little interest other than profits in the operations. Through a failure to recognize the necessity of establishing some 'center-lines' in company policy, the Board nearly stymied the Plans Committee."

The criticisms listed below are illustrative of those most frequently encountered in this study. These criticisms generally seem to be symptoms rather than causes of malfunctioning. Whether or not they are warranted, it is significant that they have appeared.

Directors are complacent and not deeply concerned over their responsibilities; they lack a profound interest in corporate welfare. "Stuffed shirts."

Directors, irrespective of whether they are executives or nonexecutives, are not independent; they often fail to have the stockholders' point of view. "Rubber stamps."

The selection and election of directors are not controlled by stockholders but by executive officers. The president may be re-elected by men whom he placed in office.

Executive-directors are more interested in "back-scratching" and "logrolling" for individual projects than in the welfare of the company as a whole.

Many directors give too little time to their duties and even fail to attend meetings regularly or to meet their most perfunctory obligations.

Directors do not know what their duties are. "They are mainly façade or window dressing."

Directors often take a narrow view of their responsibilities and neglect completely stockholders whom they are supposed to represent. Directors own no stock, or too few shares to be interested as stockholders.

Directors act on problems about which they have too little knowledge.

The directorate is just a place to which to "promote" super-annuated officers. Directors do not retire when their usefulness is over.

Directors frequently make decisions in which they are personally interested. This permits self-dealing and creates a conflict of personal interests with their responsibilities to stockholders.

Directors are recruited for the most part from a small group of influential individuals; certain directors are on a large number of directorates. They therefore tend to represent this group of persons and their thinking rather than the stockholders or the public. "Members of an exclusive club who conform to a social pattern."

Many directors know well the operations of a specific company, and are motivated by what they can "get out" of their position rather than by a desire to serve all stockholders and society effectively. The motivation of directors has never been clearly explained or understood.

Outside (nonexecutive) directors permit the establishment of groups of interlocking directors.

Directors and officers are insiders and form a self-perpetuating management group. They have great economic power, and stockholders and society have too little control over them.

The purpose of including these illustrations of criticisms at some length is not to endorse or refute them. Criticisms as well as new laws and regulations with unascertainable legal and financial liabilities have made it increasingly difficult to secure able directors, particularly for small and little-known companies. Certain directors in the early 1940's were spending time considering such questions as these: "How can I be freed from liability?" and "Is this a safe step to take?" rather than "How can I help to make the company successful?" The opinion existed in some circles either that directorates needed drastic reform or that they could, in their present form, be dispensed with entirely. Whether or not these attitudes are warranted, their existence is a real part of the directors' environment.

When those making criticisms[1] suggest corrections, their answers are frequently contradictory; they fail to appreciate the fundamental issues involved; and the suggestions, if adopted, may lead to more complications than already exist. Frequent reference to the "representative philosophy" of having a director represent a large stockholder, an association of small stockholders, customers, or some other group indicates misunderstanding of the most important function of directors, which is balancing the interests of all groups — seeing the business as a whole. It often is suggested that directors should be forced to attend board meetings regularly or be penalized for not doing so. Others suggest that directors should be paid; in this way the abuses would be avoided and better directors secured. Still others urge that to avoid these criticisms and to improve conditions, American corporations should follow English practice,[2] but when interrogated as to what English practice is, they have no adequate explanation.

Legislation is being contemplated by several groups. For example, a bill[3] introduced in the Senate in January, 1945, by Senator O'Mahoney set up standards covering corporate directors and their functions, regulating, among other things, their outside affiliations, obligations to own stock, compensation, trusteeship obligations, attendance at meetings, reports to stockholders, and their civil liabilities.

Another approach to correcting the situation was stated by an executive of long and successful experience: "It has also been my observation that to a very large extent competition takes care of this problem of management's going to seed or becoming self-serving. Corporations, like other human institutions that last for a long time, have a way of going down hill

---

[1] For a responsible summary of one critical line of complaint against the system of directors and suggested remedies, see William O. Douglas, "Directors Who Do Not Direct," *Harvard Law Review*, June, 1934, p. 1305.

[2] In contrast, one English paper, pointing to the virility of American business compared with the English, stated: "One reason for this state of affairs lies in the extent to which British business management is still dominated by the amateur. It is only in this country that the curious profession of the 'director of companies' still exists. There are thousands of men in this country who make a handsome living by sitting on a large number of boards and directing the affairs of companies to no one of which they can give more than a small fraction of their time and attention." *The Economist*, October 7, 1944, p. 469.

[3] Seventy-ninth Congress, First Session, S. 10, January 6, 1945.

and then being revolutionized and revitalized. I think it is too much to hope that any type of organization or formula of board membership can insure the constantly upward and onward movement of every corporation."

Certainly no panacea exists for magically producing able and independent directors. These critical comments can be useful, however, for they indicate the pitfalls into which boards may slip if they fail to play their full part in corporate management.

"Inside" and "Outside" Directors, Misleading Categories

The one most actively discussed subject at the time this study was made concerned "inside," or executive, directors and "outside," or nonexecutive, directors. The following statement of a stockholder quoted from a report of R. H. Macy & Company's annual stockholders' meeting in October, 1943, is pertinent: "Mr. Chairman, I notice that we have lost one of our nonemployee directors this last year and now are down to only three directors who are nonemployees, which in my opinion, is a very sad situation. . . . Too much management domination of a Board of Directors is not good for any company." The complexity of the problem is also shown by this quotation, which suggests that inherent in the question is the number of outside board members on any directorate required to satisfy critical stockholders.

Back of the simple issue, however, are important fundamental questions of human nature, which are discussed in the section of this study summarizing criticisms. Certain stockholders believed that, human nature being what it is, executives in the position of directors cannot be self-critical in an effective way and should not be placed in a position of self-dealing or making decisions which involve conflicts of personal interest with the interests of a company. Such reasoning, although sound so far as it goes, fails to take into account certain other factors affecting a director, such as his competence, knowledge of a company's technical problems, undivided loyalty, interest, and incentive. It assumes that simply through having outside representatives, ideal or at least better directorates will be secured. To analyze these issues properly, it is necessary to restate two points: (a) the objective of directors is the successful operation of a company from the broadest viewpoint; (b) the size, tradition, business problems, board policies, company organization, and numerous other factors are significant in decisions concerning the composition of a board. As in other corporate problems, there may be numerous answers rather than one. Reducing the various problems of directors and their functions to this issue of inside vs. outside directors is misleading.

Instead of two clearly defined categories of inside and outside directors, investigation revealed there were so many variations of these two classifications that classifications tended to signify little. The study revealed that no one favored all outsiders on a board, although in certain companies, such as the General Electric Company, only two executives were members of the board.[1] On the other hand, it was difficult to decide what comprised a board of insiders. For instance, one board of nine members included eight executives and the company's general counsel. In another company, with a board of eight, there were six executives plus the general counsel and a banker with numerous close business ties. Then there was the company with eleven directors, five of whom were executives and the other six personal friends of the president. When the McKesson and Robbins Company trouble occurred, its board included six outside members and twelve executives. Another board of eleven directors included three officers; the other directors were not officers but were full-time employees. Members of this board spent their full time being directors and none of them had operating responsibilities. All had had broad executive experience, and four of them had had extensive experience with other companies. These examples show that upon analysis many boards would not fall into either of the two simple[2] categories.

It should not be overlooked that many factors in the relation between directors and the administrative organization are the

[1]See Gerard Swope, "Some Aspects of Corporate Management," *Harvard Business Review*, Spring, 1945, p. 314.

(For further elaboration of reasons why there are no simple answers to the problems of directors, see George E. Bates, "The Board of Directors."

same regardless of whether the director is from inside or out-side. In the board room it is no light matter for directors to overrule administrative recommendations.

> Administration is the determination and execution of policies involving action. Such policies must be conceived by men. Such action must be effected by human organizations.[1]

Some action has to be taken, and directors cannot discharge their functions by opposing recommendations without con-tributing to constructive conclusions. Out of the board room a director has no special authority although this is sometimes forgotten. Furthermore, in seeking to find out more about problems and personnel in different departments of a corpora-tion, directors, inside or outside, must observe high standards of loyalty and business courtesy to senior officers or only con-fusion will ensue.

The problem of effective relationships between directors and executives also involves the question of the number of executives who should be on a board. Certain companies and groups of companies, as for example banks, have followed the policy of having only the president and chairman on the board. Being a board member is to most executives a real honor, and plac-ing an executive on a board may be more effective in holding him than a large salary, bonus payments, or a stock participation plan. Also having more officers on the board than the two senior men permits a wider interpretation of board action at lower echelons, may increase free discussion of policies at board meetings if vice presidents present controversial policy issues, and may add to the board men who have detailed knowledge of divisional and departmental operations. The disadvantages, in addition to those mentioned elsewhere, are apparent: discrimination among officers and the chance that these men will not be independent but vote with the senior executives and only present data and a point of view approved by their superiors. The whole subject of the selection of direc-tors is beyond the scope of this book.

[1]Wallace Brett Donham, "The Theory and Practice of Administration," *Harvard Business Review*, Summer, 1936, p. 405.

The underlying concern involved in the discussions seems to be the need for able and independent directors with high regard for their position as trustees for stockholders and society. Many advocates of outside directors assume that an outsider will be more independent, will have an "outside" point of view, and will be more interested in the welfare of stockholders than an inside director who is otherwise equally well qualified. Such men might be subservient to the president or other executives. The counterargument points out frequent instances where outside directors have gone onto the board primarily through friendship for the president. Charges of logrolling and back-scratching are leveled occasionally against both types of boards.

Independence of directors is not so much a question of whether they are inside or outside directors as it is a question of the relative dominance of the president or any one group. This will be discussed further under the subject of chairman of the board, Chapter IX. However, the following quotation from one widely experienced observer illustrates the impossibility of relating the quality of independence to any one kind of board.

> The biggest criticism of an operating board is that operating management builds up a self-perpetuating dynasty and very frequently a one-man control.
>
> In my observation as a corporation lawyer I concluded that in that regard it didn't make much difference what kind of board a corporation had. Some of the most autocratic one-man organizations and some of the most arbitrary dynasties were built up in organizations whose boards were almost exclusively composed of outside people. Banks were an outstanding example of that.
>
> Above all, it gets down to a matter of the fundamental character of the people involved.

All directors on occasion face the issue of conflicting loyalties. Critics say, for example, that inside directors are in the position of setting their own salaries. Executive-directors acknowledge that this is embarrassing because they incur the suspicion of "feathering their own nests." Companies with outside directors, however, were found to have voted high salaries for executives.[1]   In one company studied the officers refused to take the higher salaries and bonus participations that outside directors urged.   Other persons indicated that outside directors also had opportunities for self-dealing in the use of confidential information and the influencing of business through interlocking directorates or reciprocity.

Other issues raised in the debate about inside and outside directors deal with the personal ability of directors and the methods of board action: that is, the outside directors' ignorance of the business, the preoccupation of inside directors with operating problems, the relative sensitiveness of inside and outside boards to external trends, and the difficulties of getting ineffective directors off the board.   There is nothing to resolve conclusively any of these issues into a general principle favoring either form of directorate.   One director concluded his comments with the statement, "I have no theories concerning boards of directors except a belief in the need for directors of ability, character, and integrity."

It is important to emphasize that the study uncovered notable instances of effective management by boards of inside directors, by boards with a majority of outside members, and by boards which could not be placed in either category.   It is equally true that companies had been badly mismanaged under various kinds of boards.   The crucial test is not the question, What is the composition of the board?   but rather, What are the character and ability of board members? and, What results has the board achieved?

This chapter indicates the complexity of directors' problems as well as the criticisms which appear when directors are misunderstood or fail to function properly.   The problems suggest that close study of specific boards in their relations to executives and stockholders must be made before a conclusion can be reached as to a board's effectiveness.

[1]One of the specific questions studied briefly was the relation between the form of directorate and executive compensation. Preliminary analysis was inconclusive, further substantiating the conclusion that on this point the form of directorate meant little.

CHAPTER III

Specific Directorates: A Case Approach

THE first two chapters of this book reveal a lack of commonly understood and accepted definitions and interpretations of the place of directors in management and society. They outline the initial findings of a study of directors and their functions based on a large number of interviews with directors and executives, attendance at board meetings, and examination of minute-books, by-laws, and other records. The examination of individual boards in detail also was found to be necessary to the understanding of relationships among the numerous and intricate problems of directors, their functions and contributions. Time after time the stubborn facts of a particular case exploded plausible generalizations about directors, including the author's own, and led to more thorough search for concrete evidence on directorates in action.

Wide variations were found in the practices and policies of directors in the different companies examined. These variations demonstrated the need for investigation into their causes and their relation to the environment in which the companies and their directorates had developed. In order to give evidence on actual situations, detailed case studies were prepared on four profitable corporations. With the assistance and cooperation of their managements, studies were made of The American Tobacco Company, Climax Molybdenum Company, General Foods Corporation, and Standard Oil Company (New Jersey). These cases are presented in Chapters IV through VII. Each case describes the individual framework as of 1944-1945 within which the different directorates functioned: the corporate background of history and business problems, management organization, personnel, philosophy, methods of communication between directors and executives, board meetings, and relations with stockholders.

A brief account of the process of trial and error by which this approach was developed may help to emphasize the need for care in generalizing about directors. The author and associates held several preliminary planning conferences with outstanding directors in several corporations. On the basis of this preliminary survey and previous background the author prepared a broad outline of the subject. This was not a questionnaire, but a guide to the field. Subsequent interviews with more than 150 directors and executives from almost as many companies seemed to confirm the value of the preliminary outline as an index of the problem; the general social, political, and industrial environment in which directors functioned; factors in the selection, election, and development of directors; existing criticisms of directors; the vital statistics of directors composing boards, including age, years of service, and interlocking relationships; motivation, payment, and retirement; and a host of theories on representation of pressure groups and other "improvements."

The limitations of this outline, however, emerged when the wealth of data accumulated was classified according to the various subheadings; the resulting data in the various categories were disappointing and conflicting. What had been a vital, compelling line of reasoning in an interview often became just meaningless fragments when subdivided to fit into a formal outline. The results of this analysis proved to be not the discovery of an ideal pattern, but the need for tailor-made adaptation of individual boards to their own problems and personalities.

Thereupon the approach became that of seeking the factors that revealed most clearly the individuality of board functioning in specific cases. The four case studies that follow illustrate this approach.

These actual cases represent a variety of industries and sizes of company as well as a variety of types of directorates which have achieved profitable operation. Chapter VIII, Comparisons, deals more thoroughly with these contrasts and comparisons, but also shows the limited extent to which generalizations can be drawn. The managements of the four companies simply furnished information. They did not concern themselves with, nor are they responsible for, the selection of the data used, the presentation, or the conclusions reached.

If free enterprise is desirable and if it deserves to flourish, then one may well ask the question, "Who are the trustees of private enterprise for society?" If these trustees are corporate directors, and there is no other group in view, then the importance of understanding directors emerges into its proper perspective. Directors in conjunction with executive officers are responsible for the successful operation of our corporations, including earnings and dividends for stockholders, and jobs and adequate wages for employees. Too little has been known about the duties, practices, and contributions of directors as they actually function in specific companies. To throw light on reality is the purpose of the following chapters.

CHAPTER IV

The American Tobacco Company

*The American Tobacco Company board, made up of 17 company
executives, provides the study with a concrete case as setting for discussion of popular theories about so-called inside directorates.*

SOON after the Civil War, Mr. Washington Duke went to Durham, North Carolina, with his wife and three sons, and established a tobacco business. Mr. Duke manufactured his own
tobacco products, and with the assistance of his sons peddled it
in surrounding communities under the brand, Pro Bono Publico.
Later he manufactured and sold a new blend, Duke's Mixture.
The youngest son, Mr. James Buchanan Duke, left the family
plant in Durham, went to New York City, and started a cigarette business there. By 1890, he had exploited two brands of
his own so successfully that he was chosen president of the newly
formed The American Tobacco Company, a merger of the
business of W. Duke Sons & Company with four other manufacturers. The youngest Duke had achieved his success by an
aggressive promotional campaign. One feature of this was to
include in each package either coupons to be redeemed for
various articles or pictures of actresses and prize fighters. It
was estimated that Duke spent 20% of his sales on advertising.

In May, 1911, the Supreme Court of the United States ruled
that The American Tobacco Company was a monopoly operating in violation of the Sherman Anti-Trust Act, and remanded
the case to the Circuit Court of New York for further action.
A formal decree of this Court was issued in November, 1911,
ordering dissolution. For the new companies established to
take over the assets of the company, some of the old names in the
tobacco industry were revived, including Liggett & Myers
Tobacco Company and P. Lorillard Company, Inc. The American Tobacco Company name was continued, but the corporation's assets were reduced to a level comparable with that of

the other new companies. The brands of each of the various types of tobacco products were distributed among the newly formed companies in order to encourage competition and to prevent one company from having monopoly control of any one type of tobacco product.

After the dissolution, The American Tobacco Company elected Mr. Percival S. Hill as president. He had been intimately associated with Mr. Duke in various executive positions in the company since 1890. The new company at that time elected as vice president Mr. George Washington Hill.

In 1910, over 67% of the tobacco leaf processed in this country was used in the manufacture of smoking and chewing tobacco and snuff, 25% in cigars, and approximately 6% in cigarettes. After that time these proportions were drastically changed. For The American Tobacco Company the output for 1943 was divided approximately as follows: cigarettes, 93%; smoking and chewing tobaccos, 4%; and cigars, 3%. During the period from 1911 to 1944, national consumption of cigarettes increased from 10 billion to 322 billion a year.

The history of the tobacco companies of the United States after 1911 is, in part, a history of the changing tastes of the American public. The tastes did not shift abruptly but were diverted by advertising and by changes in consumers' tobacco habits. Competition was keen. The American Tobacco Company came into the burley blend cigarette business after other companies had already established brand names. Many brands held frequent advertising campaigns. Sales leadership alternated among a few strong brands as producers changed advertising programs.

The American Tobacco Company had spent considerable effort and money in advertising its smoking tobacco, Bull Durham. And beginning in 1918, it used national billboard advertising for its leading 15-cent cigarette brand, Lucky Strike, and inaugurated a nationwide newspaper advertising campaign to increase sales of Lucky Strikes. In subsequent years the promotional material included the use of testimonials on a large scale for the first time, and inaugurated the "Reach for a Lucky instead of a Sweet" slogan. This appeal was directed to women and, executives believed, it contributed in part to the increase in their consumption of cigarettes. During the early Lucky campaigns the company used all kinds of media in addition to newspapers. It used the radio extensively and later increased its use of this medium.[1]

The advertising program of The American Tobacco Company was part of an extensive distribution plan. The company employed salesmen to visit jobbers, wholesalers, and retailers. Ordinarily sales were made only to wholesalers and jobbers. Despite the fact that the company did not sell directly to retailers, however, the salesmen visited some 900,000 retail outlets at frequent intervals. Most of their work with retailers consisted of arranging counter displays and dealer helps, demonstrating by samples and illustrations, inquiring about retailers' complaints or customers' complaints relayed through the retailer, and otherwise attempting to retain the goodwill of the retailer and consumers. In certain retail outlets selected by the manufacturer window displays were provided once a month.

To maintain high quality of product for the wide market thus cultivated, The American Tobacco Company sent buyers each year to the leading tobacco auction markets in the South. In the fall these men purchased in the markets as they opened from Georgia north to Virginia. In smaller markets, when a buyer was unable to be present at the opening, orders were placed with leaf dealers. Most domestic tobacco was bought direct from the farmer, redried, and then stored in hogsheads. The company also imported Turkish leaf tobacco.

The details of manufacture in the tobacco business have been of critical importance. Expert tobacco men were apparently unable to describe fully the art of which they were masters. Just as was true of the creation of many articles that have to do with taste and the human palate, so in the case of tobaccos it was in the creation of formulae and in the details of handling blends and in the processes employed that the skill of the tobacco manufacturer was demonstrated. Variations

[1]The importance of advertising in the development of the tobacco industry is illustrated in *The Economic Effects of Advertising*, by Neil H. Borden (Chicago, Richard D. Irwin, Inc., 1942), Chapter VIII, "The Effect of Advertising on the Demand for Tobacco Products—Cigarettes" and Chapter IX, "The Effect of Advertising on the Demand for Cigars and Smoking Tobacco."

in this skill were wide, and volume maintenance of a blend which had a broad public appeal was of tremendous influence in popularizing the brand under which it was sold. The company emphasized throughout its plants, "Quality of product is essential to *continuing success.*"

By 1943, annual sales were $529,422,000[1] with profits of $22,534,000. In 1912, after the dissolution, sales were $67,-950,000 and profits, $12,243,000. Dividends were paid consistently. Capital stock and surplus, which had a balance sheet value of $133,250,650 at the end of 1912, had increased to $224,455,400 at the end of 1943. Funds from rights in 1929 amounted to $48,980,400. Three classes of stock were outstanding in 1943: 526,997 shares of 6% $100 par preferred having 4 votes per share; 1,515,983 shares of voting common stock; and 2,966,012 shares of nonvoting common B stock. There were 73,517 shareholders of all classes of stock; this number had increased by 43,280 since 1929. There were some 19,000 employees.

Top Management Organization — Directors and Executives

The directors and their principal executive positions are shown in Exhibit 2, with the year each was first elected to the board and the number of shares of stock owned, as reported in the proxy statement issued March 1, 1944. The directors owned 0.38% of voting privileges.

Mr. Hill described the functions of the president and directors as follows: "As president of The American Tobacco Company, I am responsible to the directors and to the stockholders for the operation of all departments of the company and all of the company's activities. The American Tobacco Company is operated as a team. We have 17 directors. Each director is actively identified with the company and has commercially no outside interest. He devotes all of his time to the company. We have no outside directors.

"Under the by-laws, the directors are authorized by the stockholders to elect a president and not more than five vice presidents annually. During my administration, at most times I have operated with four vice presidents.

[1]Includes Federal revenue stamps affixed to the products for 1943, $279,069,763.

EXHIBIT 2. THE AMERICAN TOBACCO COMPANY: INFORMATION
REGARDING DIRECTORS

Name	Year First Elected Director	Shares Owned Common (Voting)	Shares Owned Common (Nonvoting)	Preferred (4 votes a share)
George W. Hill President	1912	3,712	2,331	80
Paul M. Hahn Vice President	1931	1,405		
George W. Hill, Jr. Vice President, on leave of absence for Military Service	1936	4	1,800	200
Vincent Riggio Vice President	1927	3,745	40	
James E. Lipscomb, Jr. President, American Suppliers, Inc.	1918	1,200	300	100
Orpheus D. Baxalys Vice President, The American Tobacco Company of the Orient, Inc.	1940	540	130	32
Richard J. Boylan Secretary	1929	101		
James R. Coon Auditor	1936	160		50
John A. Crowe Assistant Chief of Manufacture	1931		187	5
Preston L. Fowler Chief of Manufacture	1941	100		
C. Huntley Gibson Branch Manager	1930	101		
Patrick H. Gorman President, The American Tobacco Company of the Orient, Inc.	1931	201	50	
Hiram R. Hanmer Director of Research	1938	100		
Edmund A. Harvey Treasurer	1932		140	40
Harry L. Hilyard Assistant Treasurer	1944	100		
William H. Ogsbury Assistant Chief of Manufacture	1930		100	50
Fred B. Reuter Assistant Auditor and Assistant Treasurer	1931	21	160	

SOURCE: Proxy Statement, March 1, 1944.

EXHIBIT 3. THE AMERICAN TOBACCO COMPANY
Condensed Organization Chart as of July 1, 1944

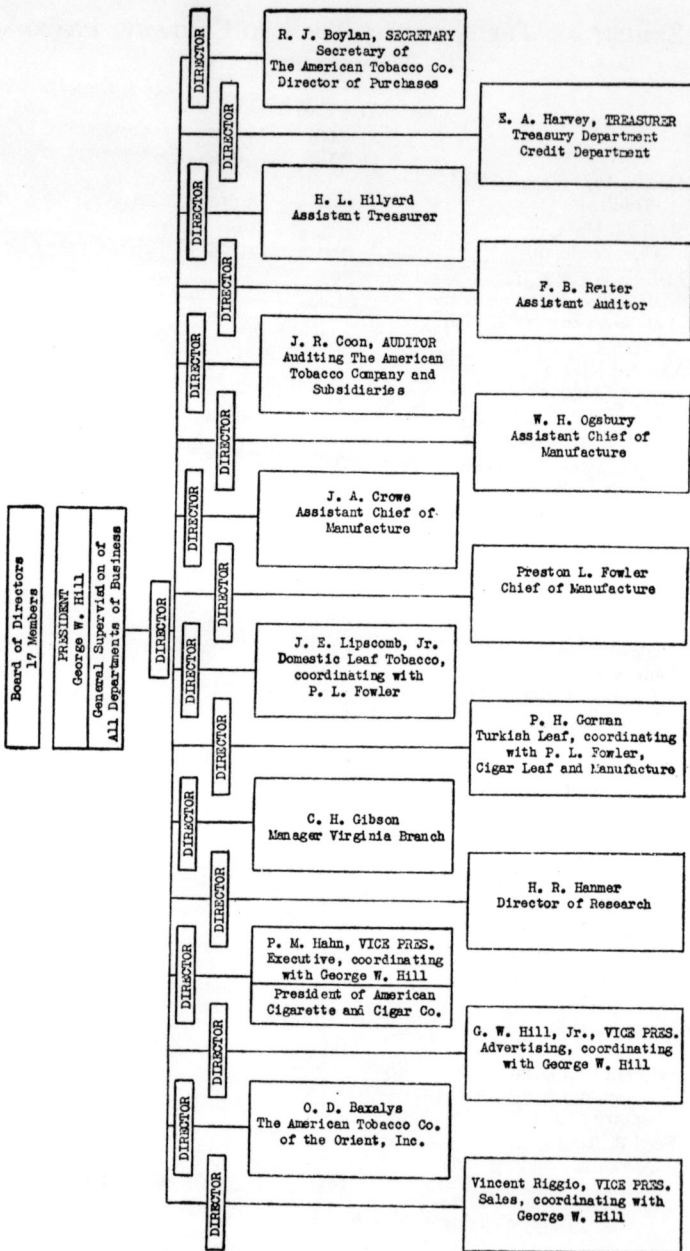

Board of Directors
17 Members

PRESIDENT
George W. Hill
General Supervision of
All Departments of Business

DIRECTOR — R. J. Boylan, SECRETARY
Secretary of
The American Tobacco Co.
Director of Purchases

DIRECTOR — E. A. Harvey, TREASURER
Treasury Department
Credit Department

DIRECTOR — H. L. Hilyard
Assistant Treasurer

DIRECTOR — F. B. Reuter
Assistant Auditor

DIRECTOR — J. R. Coon, AUDITOR
Auditing The American
Tobacco Company and
Subsidiaries

DIRECTOR — W. H. Ogsbury
Assistant Chief of
Manufacture

DIRECTOR — J. A. Crowe
Assistant Chief of
Manufacture

DIRECTOR — Preston L. Fowler
Chief of Manufacture

DIRECTOR — J. E. Lipscomb, Jr.
Domestic Leaf Tobacco,
coordinating with
P. L. Fowler

DIRECTOR — P. H. Gorman
Turkish Leaf, coordinating
with P. L. Fowler,
Cigar Leaf and Manufacture

DIRECTOR — C. H. Gibson
Manager Virginia Branch

DIRECTOR — H. R. Hanmer
Director of Research

DIRECTOR — P. M. Hahn, VICE PRES.
Executive, coordinating
with George W. Hill
President of American
Cigarette and Cigar Co.

DIRECTOR — G. W. Hill, Jr., VICE PRES.
Advertising, coordinating
with George W. Hill

DIRECTOR — O. D. Baxalys
The American Tobacco Co.
of the Orient, Inc.

DIRECTOR — Vincent Riggio, VICE PRES.
Sales, coordinating with
George W. Hill

[36]

"Each of our directors holds an important position in the activities of the company. He is in an executive position, manager of a factory or some department. It is my business to work with the directors, to see that each director's department is operating properly and efficiently, and that the coordination of the directors in their total effort builds business and develops the business of The American Tobacco Company." The company maintained a book of formal organization charts showing the lines of responsibility for each director. The chart of directorate and management is abbreviated as Exhibit 3.

The American Tobacco Company had had outside directors and a chairman of the board for a period following the sudden death of Mr. Percival S. Hill on December 7, 1925. The board of directors elected Mr. George Washington Hill as president and created the position of chairman of the board, to which they elected Mr. Junius Parker, who had been general counsel. Mr. Parker was also elected president of the American Cigar Company, a partially-owned subsidiary. At this same meeting of The American Tobacco Company board, vacancies were filled by election of Mr. James H. Perkins, president of Farmers Loan and Trust Company, and Mr. Donald Geddes, of Clark, Dodge and Company. On May 1, 1929, Mr. Parker resigned from both his positions to return to the practice of law. On April 3, 1930, executives from three large manufacturing centers of The American Tobacco Company were elected in place of the outside directors.

In recent years the management followed the policy of selecting directors from the executive staff in recognition of their contribution to the successful operation of the company. Election as a director was considered a great honor and worth more than money, according to one director. Another director stated that as a director he had no responsibilities outside his particular department, other than the responsibility of voting upon those matters which came before him in a directors' meeting. There was no tradition automatically assuring election to the board upon promotion to any executive position except the presidency or vice presidency. The president explained how carefully he and the other directors considered an individual's qualifications when selecting a new director. He consulted with senior directors and with the department head when they were considering a subordinate. Because of the care used in selecting men for the directorate, the president could not recall any instance when a director had not measured up to requirements.

Following the rigid policy of keeping directors to a closely knit, inside group did not mean that the management was unaware of outside points of view and the value of criticism, according to Mr. Hill. He stated that "located as our factories are in southern communities, largely self-contained, we feel it is a definite advantage to our people to have the privilege of participating in discussions with expert consultants and in meeting with other representatives of industry, to the end that the broader problems of administration from various points of view come to our people's attention, and that their own point of view be broadened thereby."

The most vital function of the management, directors and executives, was building business, in the opinion of The American Tobacco Company directors. "Stewardship and trusteeship were inherent in the election of the right men as directors," Mr. Hill commented. "Our prescription for building business has been expressed in the mottoes: 'Quality of product is essential to *continuing success*.' 'It is the desire and policy of The American Tobacco Company to extend to its customers the maximum of service and every courtesy within its power'." "A cigarette is just a little tobacco wrapped up in a piece of paper; quality of product makes it a good smoke," according to Mr. Hill, and "It is up to management to breathe into the product the imagination[1] to get people to ask for it." He added that, "From the point of view of the stockholders, the owners of the business, our practices are and have been sound, and although we seek no credit for it they have been sound from the point of view of the average citizen. I mean by that, we have built a great and growing industry with consequent beneficial result to producers and consumers alike, and while no man or

[1]"And this story of American Tobacco is a story of phrases rather than factories or processes or farmers or even salesmen. . . . Not toasting but 'It's toasted' is the key to American Tobacco." "The American Tobacco Co.," *Fortune*, December, 1936, p. 98.

company can claim maximum credit for the performance, there is no question but what my company has been in the van in the development of the tobacco business. Business administration (the successful development of business and all that goes with it) is all important for the future of our country and our people."

Methods of Communication

Mr. Hill illustrated one of the techniques of communication within the organization in explaining how he kept before executives the basic principle: "Quality of product is essential to continuing success." "This is an axiom that it becomes my duty as President to emphasize almost daily in my contact with various directors and heads of departments. This definite evaluation on our balance sheet[1] [brands, trade-marks, patents, goodwill, etc.... $54,099,431.40] has enabled me for years to emphasize to our people in all departments the importance of a continuation of careful scrutiny of quality. It's a much more simple matter to visualize to your buyer of leaf tobacco the importance of buying good tobacco when you have physically before you the evidence that $54,000,000 of the company's money is invested in the intangible public acceptance of the goodwill of your product."

Another illustration of the way director-executives carried the policies of the company down into operations ànd learned of current developments was explained in the following extract from a letter written by Mr. Hill to stockholders, October 2, 1939, about Mr. Lipscomb. As a director and president of the leaf tobacco buying subsidiary, American Suppliers, Inc., Mr. Lipscomb was responsible for leaf purchases, which made up a large part of the inventory carried at $236,167,930 on the December 31, 1943, balance sheet. "I have been on the markets many times with Mr. Lipscomb in South Carolina, North Carolina, Virginia, and Kentucky. I have just returned from a

[1]Mr. Hill called attention to "Accounting for Intangible Assets," *Accounting Research Bulletins*, No. 24, December, 1944, issued by the Committee on Accounting Procedure, American Institute of Accountants, New York, 1944: "(3) The cost of type (b) intangibles [goodwill, trade names, and secret processes, for example] may be carried continuously unless and until it becomes reasonably evident that the term of existence of such intangibles has become limited, or that they have become worthless...."

trip with him to Virginia and North Carolina and will be with him on the markets in Kentucky in January. As Mr. Lipscomb visits his buyers, it is his custom to this day to relieve the actual buyer on the market, taking on two, three or four rows of tobacco in open competition with the fifteen or twenty regular buyers operating for other companies. When he has made his purchases, he, his assistants and the local buyer go over them, pile by pile. Our local buyer is encouraged to criticize Mr. Lipscomb's judgment both as to the quality of tobacco purchased and the grade into which he has put that tobacco."

This dual communication of policies and problems between the working director-executives and the operating organization is illustrated in another letter written by the president to stockholders on January 2, 1940, about Mr. Riggio, director and vice president in charge of sales. Both these letters are taken from a series Mr. Hill wrote to the stockholders about key executives and their part in the management of the company. The other letters in the series were in similar vein.

"These records show that, during one hundred and forty-one days out of the three hundred and sixty-five, Vincent Riggio, for the past ten years Vice President in Charge of Sales of The American Tobacco Company, was out on the road, from Maine to California, from Jacksonville to Seattle, visiting with his men, working with them, showing them how to do a better job, and at the same time maintaining contact with the Company's thousands of direct customers.

"He is a worker. Even to this day, he can take one side of the street as a retail sales-service man, and work rings around the regular man on the job.

"There is nothing of the 'stuffed shirt' about this man. He has never forgotten the importance of the small retailer. He says 'Thank you' today when he sees an order for 100 cigarettes with just as much sincerity as he says 'Thank you' for an order for ten million—because he knows that it is the many little orders of 100 each, received from the 900,000 merchants who sell tobacco products throughout this country, that bring the many orders for ten million that come, each day, into the offices of the Company."

During World War II, The American Tobacco Company

started publishing "*Sold American*," a bimonthly brochure which it sent to all employees in the service and all other employees. The objectives were stated as follows:

A. It is intended to inculcate in each and every employee, and most especially our factory employees, a pride on their part in the quality of manufacture by repeating the *fact* that "Quality of product is essential to *continuing success.*"

B. It is intended to demonstrate that each and every employee of The American Tobacco Company is dependent one upon the other. Any mistake, any error, any carelessness injures not only the guilty individual but each and every other employee of the Company.

The spirit of "*Sold American*" should be warm and friendly because after all we are all going to prosper or not prosper dependent upon how well we all get along together. Cooperation is the keynote. Loyalty to the Company is to be cherished and engendered through the mutual respect, trust and friendship that are built up through constant daily business association in our efforts to feed, clothe and shelter ourselves. The Company is the means toward that most important end.

Each issue of the brochure aimed at relating historical "commercials" selected from the company's radio programs with the stated objectives. This series of commercials was based on dramatic characters and events from early American history.

Board Meetings and Minutes and Problems Submitted to the Board

The board met each week, but often there was no business to be transacted and the meeting adjourned. The following items illustrate the subjects dealt with and the action taken at board meetings during the course of the year, as indicated by the minutes.

Approved salary increases. These were based on recommendations by department heads, approval by president and a member of the Committee on Salary and Wage Increases, and a statement that the increases conformed to the schedule approved by the Salary Stabilization Unit of the Internal Revenue Department.

Approved depository bank.

Approved proxies for subsidiaries.

Officially designated corporate agent to qualify in certain states.

Amended By-Laws to provide for holding annual meeting at city of principal office at a different time and place.

Assistant treasurer reported discounting and renewing bank notes.

Declared dividends.

Authorized payments to old employees per Committee on Payments.

Named proxies and place of annual stockholders' meeting.

Approved recommendation of auditor for employing independent C.P.A. firm.

Authorized officers to sign papers for Collector of Internal Revenue.

Elected a director to fill vacancy by death.

Approved Memorial Minute.

Authorized ration bank account.

Approved action of officers on salaries of $3,500 a year or under, per list of the auditor submitted by the secretary.

Appointed C.P.A. firm members as inspectors of election.

Approved annual report and report of C.P.A.

Approved proxy notice and statement.

Approved salaries. This action covered a large number of annual increases under the schedule approved by the Salary Stabilization Unit of the Collector of Internal Revenue.

Established reserve against investments of doubtful value.

Approved registration statement for new debenture issue.

Authorized officers to sign registration statement.

Approved indenture for new debenture issue.

Appointed temporary assistant treasurers and assistant secretaries for the sole purpose of signing the debentures.

Authorized application for listing the debentures on the New York Stock Exchange.

Received report of purchase of stock of subsidiary minority interest.

Authorized issuance of new stock certificate to replace one lost.

Directors' Methods of Handling Problems

Mr. Hill characterized formal directors' meetings as "the slow way to meet problems that require prompt action. Our business is current. I have had three meetings with individual directors this morning on their particular phases of the business in which there were problems. We discuss all important policy matters with our directors in our directors' meetings, but we gain prompt action by daily contact with those men who know and are trained in each specific branch of the business that daily presents its problems."

Mr. Hill stated that The American Tobacco Company adapted itself promptly and effectively to circumstances through its "working directorate." He illustrated this in the following letter, which he sent to every member of the board of directors and to all key men of his organization, enclosing a series of tables and charts entitled "Domestic Sales and Advertising Expenditures of the Three Leading Brands of Cigarettes," compiled by Charles D. Mitchell of the New York office of The Curtis Publishing Company.

"I recently received a letter from Lt. Everard W. Meade, USNR, your friend and mine and our former associate. Lt. Meade is located somewhere in the Pacific doing his job with the Navy. He is undoubtedly an example of thousands of our employees presently in the service. His point of view and attitude towards the Company and towards a postwar job and opportunity are I would think typical of that of our other employees in the service. I quote from Lt. Meade's letter to me.

> I am inclined to think of the future as a time of opportunity and expanding trade, a time when a sadder and wiser nation moves towards maturity. From a narrow personal viewpoint, sitting here melting a starched khaki collar, I think of it as a period that begins when a ship or plane raises the outline of California and a train pulls into a station crowded with searching faces. Beyond that (barring a return to the Pacific) a resumption of family life and then — finally — the great day when the moth army of occupation is driven out of the tweed suits and life really begins to click.
>
> Moving a step beyond that, one's thoughts reach the day of rejoining the Tobacco Company and the excitement of productive confabs and the association of all of us in the interest of the stockholders, a stewardship not without amusement and profit for each of us.
>
> It is a good company to work for. For some reason, you have worked so hard and for such a long time to make it exactly that, I feel that you might forgive the obviousness of such a statement on the part of an overseas employee in a mood of

admitted nostalgia. There must be several thousand who would agree; where they are I have no idea, scattered clear around the world, I suppose.

Certainly one of Mr. Riggio's men would agree, remembering that his equipment excelled his competitors, that his training was hard but fair, his salary generous, his opportunity for advancement dependent upon no one but himself and his ability to do the job.

Certainly one of Preston Fowler's men would agree, remembering factories run with efficiency and consideration, hospital benefits, fair wages, good working conditions.

Certainly the tobaccomen who bought leaf for Mr. Lipscomb would agree, remembering years of continual search for quality, remembering fair practice in a competitive market, remembering Mr. Lipscomb himself working the sales with his coat off and his heart in his business.

This, of course, is as familiar to you as the taste of a Lucky. Indeed, you may wonder why I have set it down in so many words. Well, I am not sure; primarily it is because I simply wanted to. I am not speaking for the others, just for myself. I make no pretense of knowing what Fritz Wilhelmi is thinking cramped up in a Berlin-bound tank. But I have a hunch about Fritz, and about the others. I have a hunch their feelings are pretty much like mine; *let's get it over and get back to work.*

"'*Let's get back to work,*' and that goes for all of us, those who are presently at work and those who will return. But in the interest of our Company and to our own satisfaction let us seek in every branch of the business to make our work ultra-productive.

"I enclose herewith for your attention a copy of a survey of the three leading brands of cigarettes independently compiled by the Saturday Evening Post people and covering a period of 10 years' operations. This survey covers advertising expenditures, comparative, in radio time, in newspapers and in magazines, and emphasizes The American Tobacco Company's policy of concentration of expenditures. It will repay study on your part.

"Adding up the figures reported in the survey for the 10-year period shows that the average advertising expenditure of The American Tobacco Company in radio time, newspapers and magazines on the sale of one thousand LUCKY STRIKE Cigarettes was 12.7 cents; the same average of the R. J. Reynolds Tobacco Company on the sale of one thousand Camel Cigarettes was 19.0 cents; the same average of the Liggett & Myers Tobacco Company on the sale of one thousand Chesterfield Cigarettes was 22.9 cents. And, I repeat, these averages cover a period of 10 years.

"As in sales and advertising, *so in every department of our business we must strive to surpass and exceed*, in efficiency of intelligent operation, our competition. *The success of our Company depends on such an attitude and on such an accomplishment by each and every one of us.* We who head up The American Tobacco Company, we who are responsible in the various departments, all branches of the Company's operations, must see to it that present employees and returned employees all strive to perform their jobs with energy, with enthusiasm, with pride of accomplishment and of production. On the record our employees know that the Company will care for them if they deliver the goods. *It's our job as executives to see that the goods are delivered, and enthusiastically delivered by every employee in the Company's service.*

"It gives me pleasure to furnish you with this comparative record of ten years of the Company's operations, a record compiled without any suggestion on our part by the Saturday Evening Post people. It is my duty to urge you in your department and with the matters under your control to see that some such comparative record attaches itself to your operations, even though you may not be so fortunate as to have the direct comparison furnished to you."

Mr. Hill stated that the approach to advertising was one illustration of the directors' constant objective of making money for the stockholders. During World War II, with rising prices of leaf tobacco, ceiling prices on cigarettes, and the general increases in costs of operation and distribution, the margin of profit for stockholders began to shrink. Concluding that action had to be taken, Mr. Hill talked the problem over with Mr. Riggio, director and vice president in charge of sales, and one or two other directors who had particular concern with that phase of the business. They agreed not to try to compete with Uncle Sam for salesmen or to spend a lot of money in advertising the restricted volume of cigarettes available to civilians. Therefore they set as an objective the maintenance of the company's competitive position with an advertising budget cut by many millions of dollars. The percentage of sales budgeted for advertising already had been reduced to a fraction of the 20% reputedly used for advertising by James B. Duke. In the absence of Mr. George W. Hill, Jr., vice president in charge of advertising, on leave for service in the armed forces, Mr. George W. Hill took direct responsibility for developing a program to meet these objectives. He explained that there was no use in taking up the time of the whole board on a thing of this sort, which, after all, required specialized knowledge.

As one step toward the objective of making the advertising budget effective while keeping it within a margin that would leave profits for stockholders, Mr. Hill addressed the problem to each member of outside advertising agencies employed and to all directors and members of The American Tobacco Company organization who were qualified in this field. Mr. Hill had had previous meetings with a smaller group, in which agreement had been worked out as to the imperative need for a "formula" in all advertising and particularly in the proper commercial use of radio. Mr. Hill kept before executives the formula for each advertising and selling effort, in leather binders, prefaced with the following prescription boldly superimposed over a compass on a heavy celluloid flyleaf.

THINK!

The American Tobacco Company always knows its objective in advertising — where it is going — or IT DON'T.

The latter statement is just as important as any part of this summation because if we don't know where we are going, then we recognize that that's a period of "chin chin" and through mutual discussion between the Company executives and the agency executives, all interested, we come to a definite opinion as to our objective.

It is as though we placed a compass on the desk. The needle spins around and finally stops directly north. The "chin chin" period is the period prior to the time the needle has settled and when we see the needle has settled we proceed.

The value of the formula should be stressed as being an active, motivating, guiding force, not a bureaucratic dead end. Always consider formula books as "road maps" rather than as tombstones. The principle of a formula is essentially that of change. When change fails to appear, then watch out, that is a danger signal.

> THINK..Go thru the period of "chin chin" — then *chart your course!*

After studying a number of these formula books, one outside advertising expert concluded:

> These were very revealing as to why The American Tobacco Company has surged to the top in its sale of Lucky Strike cigarettes with an expenditure which, as far as I can judge, is less than that of the other big tobacco companies.

> These volumes disclose the leadership exerted by Mr. Hill within his organization and agencies to find new and more effective ways to carry across his basic appeal to consumers. He has caused every important executive within his company and in his advertising agency to give careful study and analysis to building Lucky Strike radio commercials that impress and programs that attract.

> He has carefully studied the suggestions of these people and then with them has formed plans with clear-cut objectives. The current plan, with its unusual techniques, — the tobacco auctioneer, the LS/MFT, and the so-called "impulse tags" to drive home the product's appeals, has been adhered to over a long enough period of time to sear them into the consciousness of the American public. While the management apparently has made constant attempts to improve its programs to get better techniques for the commercials, the basic plan has been consistently adhered to. The simple fundamental of constantly driving home a sound basic idea has been followed.

> The magazine advertising program follows the same fundamental pattern as the radio program. A few forceful advertisements picturing the "glorified and glamorous" leaf of tobacco, which illustrates the basic selling message, are given intensive publication. Mr. Hill has concentrated on a limited and selected list of publications of large circulation, with simple, direct, and dramatic copy.

> I was interested to note further that this same drive in the basic appeal was carried over into window display and into the plans of the selling organization. There has been unusual coordination.

Mr. Hill studied and summarized 30 or more replies which commented on the existing formulae or suggested changes. His tentative plan for a change in commercials on the basis of some of the suggestions was abandoned when an outside consultant pointed out that the secret of The American Tobacco Company's radio success had been the use of its "inexorable logic...a syllogism repeated, expanded, repeated, inverted, repeated...and never obscured. This is the LUCKY STRIKE commercial pattern. And I do not think it wants the slightest addition." Growing out of this period of what Mr. Hill called "chin chin" emerged the "$5,000,000 advertising infield—Tinker to Evers to Chance": LS/MFT reminders on billions of Lucky Strike packages plus color magazine advertisements plus feature radio programs. Mr. Hill foresaw this formula as the solution of the budget and promotion problem.

One of the stories credited to James B. Duke by Mr. Hill bore on the directors' major job of maintaining able management. "The trouble with this business is the future," prophesied Mr. Duke. He would pound his forehead with clenched fist saying, "One man has a bump for selling." Striking the back of his head with the other fist, he declared, "Another a bump for buying." With another thump he emphasized that some other executive had a bump for manufacturing, or another, a bump for finance. "The problem is to knock all of these together into one man who can run the business. The trouble is that the job is getting so big that no one sees all the way around it." The American Tobacco Company theory of top executive promotion was to use care in selecting as directors 17 top-notch experts all having respect for each other. Mr. Hill was convinced that there was little conscious "rounding" that could or should be given to any particular specialist.

In "knocking around" among this group of directors, someone would begin to stand out as the consultant of the rest; the natural leader would rise to the top. Selection of the president was the responsibility of the board. Mr. Hill would not even make a recommendation, although from time to time he noted factors that ought to be considered by the board when the time came to pick his successor.

The determination of top management compensation was

removed in part from the directors when, at Mr. Duke's recommendation, stockholders provided for incentive compensation in the by-laws and reserved to themselves the right of amendment. The following explanation of this principle is abridged from letters written by Mr. Hill to stockholders.

"Under the plan of dissolution, Mr. Duke was to be a large stockholder in the new companies, as he had been in the old. He felt it advisable that he himself should have no part in the management of these new competitive companies, *and from a personal point of view he was greatly concerned about providing a real incentive for the men who were to run them.*

"I remember, as if it were yesterday, how Mr. Duke explained his plan to me the day he told me I had been selected to be one of the Vice Presidents of the new The American Tobacco Company. He called me into his office — the very room that is my office today — he sat in the place that I now occupy, and I sat opposite him — he wagged two fingers of his hand at me in the gesture that was typical of him, and he said:

"'George, I've worked it out: this is it. If I sat here, and there was a procession of men coming in through that door, each bringing me $100, I'd be glad to give each of them $10, because there would be $90 out of every hundred for me. If I own a business, and somebody else runs it for me, and I want additional profits, the smart thing for me to do is to make a deal with him that I'll pay him $10 out of every $100 *of the additional profit he earns for me.* If he brings me enough additional profit, he'll profit too — but I won't mind that, because I'll be getting $90 out of every hundred. Well, that's the idea I'm going to propose to the stockholders of every one of these companies. Now if you fellows sit back and are satisfied with what your business is earning now, you'll have to get along with a salary. But if you stir your stumps and increase the profits, you'll gain with the stockholders by the increase, and *your stockholders will be glad to pay it to you, because they'll get 90% of the result of your work.*'

"That was Mr. Duke's plan, and the stockholders of all the resulting tobacco companies were quick to adopt it. In our Company — The American Tobacco Company — it took the form of Article XII of the By-laws and was adopted by 621,047 shares, with only 35 shares voting against it. That Article provides, in substance, that during any year in which the Company's key officers — the President and five Vice Presidents — are able to produce in addition to the dividends on the preferred stock, net profits as therein defined in excess of such profits estimated for 1910, the Company shall pay 10% of such excess to these officers, in the proportion of $2\frac{1}{2}$% (of the excess only) to the President and $1\frac{1}{2}$% (of the excess only) to each of the Vice Presidents, as part of their salary for the year. There is only this difference between the By-law as adopted and as it is effective today: — In 1933, the officers entered into agreements with the Company whereby the point at which their By-law compensation commences was changed from approximately $11,000,000 by yearly steps to the present base of $15,500,000, and, starting at profits of $32,500,000, the percentage was graded down by blocks of $2,500,000 each to an eventual 5%. These changes take liberal account of any additional capital that has been contributed by stockholders.

"I cannot emphasize too strongly my belief that, in the Company's interest and that of its stockholders, the principles[1] which I have stated in this letter must be maintained and preserved as a Company policy. As active head of your Company I have seen these principles work; I consider them the base of the extra initiative, the exceptional quality production, the unusual economies, and the extraordinary sales expansion that have marked your Company's progress. I have held out as incentive to each of the Vice Presidents who have assisted me in my work, the benefits given him by Article XII,[2] which benefits would accrue to all of us if, working as a team, we produced continuing and notable profits for the stockholders of the Company."

The directors dealt formally with questions requiring their action as a board, as in the borrowing of funds. On April 15, 1942, the company sold $100,000,000 of 3% debentures as authorized by the board for the purpose of paying off bank

[1] The history of some of the litigation concerning compensation was summarized in the court's opinion in *Heller et al.* v. *Boylan et al.*, 29 N.Y.S. 2d 653, Special Term New York County (1941).

[2] Resolutions to amend Article XII introduced by a certain stockholder at annual meetings in 1940, 1941, and 1942 were defeated by a large majority of votes cast.

loans used for inventory purposes. During the course of the war, however, the demand for cigarettes increased so greatly that directors began to discuss the need for additional funds. Mr. Hill explained that one investment banker approached them about raising a comparatively small amount of money to pay off bank loans. The amount did not seem adequate to Mr. Hill, but the idea took hold. Later on, as he foresaw the continued expansion of demand and as the buying season approached, he held some preliminary informal discussions with Mr. Harold Stanley, of Morgan Stanley & Company, as well as with directors who were immediately concerned with the financial needs of the company. The informal discussions at The American Tobacco Company resulted in agreement on the need for $100,000,000.

After these discussions, the chief director-executives of The American Tobacco Company met with Morgan Stanley & Company. Mr. Hill told the underwriters how much money the company needed and left to them the form of financing. They suggested another issue of 3% debentures due in 25 years. Within three weeks and one day the board had met and given formal authorization to appropriate officers to file registration statements with the Securities and Exchange Commission. The board met again to authorize formally the corporate indenture and make provision for authenticating the securities, those directors who specialized in financial matters having in the meanwhile made their recommendations to Mr. Hill and to the whole board. Furthermore, within those 22 days, the filing papers were completed and filed, the underwriting arranged and advertised, and the books of subscription closed at a price of 101.

As soon as the financing had been completed, instructions were given to Mr. Lipscomb, chief tobacco buyer, to bend every effort to increase purchases to meet the expanding volume of sales.

Reports of Management to Stockholders

The annual report to stockholders was primarily a formal financial statement. It included the auditor's certificate and a brief paragraph of transmittal from the treasurer. The president wrote to all stockholders a supplemental letter discussing important developments, usually enclosing it with the annual proxy statement. The president also wrote to stockholders on other occasions. Some of the letters were quoted in earlier sections of this study. The following is a list of the material sent to stockholders in 1943.

January 27, 1943. Letter to all stockholders.

Covered extra dividend and called attention to *"the fact that our percentage of increased cigarette sales for 1942 was almost double that obtained by the balance of the industry as a whole."*

March 1, 1943.　　Letter to common and preferred stockholders re annual meeting April 7, 1943, and request for prompt execution of proxy.

Enclosed with this letter was the annual proxy statement and financial report, and proxy to be filled out and returned. The dividend checks were also sent.

April 15, 1943.　　Letter to all stockholders.

This letter explained the reason for preparing the enclosed booklet "Tobacco and War" as a means of emphasizing the contribution of employees to the war effort.

April 15, 1943.　　"Tobacco and War."

This was an illustrated booklet quoting statements by General MacArthur, George Washington, General Pershing, President Roosevelt, General Hershey, and Donald Nelson covering the importance of tobacco for morale; it was supplemented by photographs of employees at work at The American Tobacco Company plants. The booklet also carried facsimile letters from soldiers at the battlefronts, emphasizing the importance of cigarettes for morale.

May 22, 1943.　　Letter to stockholders re June 1 dividend and a carton of cigarettes.

This letter explained how stockholders could help the company by using the package of 200 Lucky Strike cigarettes to make new friends for Lucky Strike. The letter also included an advance proof of the advertisement "Tobacco Talk," a painting by the American painter, James Chapin, to appear in color in June and July magazines.

The American Tobacco Company

November 12, 1943. Letter to stockholders re December 1 dividend and a carton of cigarettes.

This letter covered the preview first edition of the Christmas package of 200 Lucky Strike cigarettes, suggesting that stockholders show this Christmas carton, in advance of its receipt by the general public, to as many friends as possible.

In other years the stockholders had been sent additional information, such as the 75-page booklet, *The American Tobacco Company and its Service to the Public*, July, 1940. This booklet explained the historical development of the company and its relation to consumers, farmers, employees, the tobacco trade, its competitors, the government, and stockholders. It concluded with an outline of the company's sales principles.

On October 25, 1941, the company sent out a tabulated estimate of how new excess profits tax legislation would affect earnings available for dividends. The president explained that this tax made it seem best to recommend a reduction in the regular dividend payable December 1, 1941.

Mr. Hill welcomed all new stockholders with a letter stating the management's belief that they were, in a sense, business partners. He also suggested a number of ways in which the stockholder could help the company, and invited constructive criticism. In addition, he sent a carton of 200 Luckies, asking that the stockholder recommend them to friends and associates. Mr. Hill reported that the stockholders responded enthusiastically and effectively.

CHAPTER V

Climax Molybdenum Company

The Climax Molybdenum Company is a significant company to include in this study because the process of stock dispersion among the public had not progressed so far in 1944-1945 as in the other three companies. One criticism against directors frequently made, that they were not large stockholders, did not apply to this company. Most of the directors, as in the early history of the company, still were large stockholders, directly or indirectly, when this study was made. Interests closely associated with the management still controlled approximately half the common stock, even though the total number of stockholders had increased to more than 7,000.

The Climax Molybdenum Company was incorporated in 1918 by a group of directors and employees in The American Metal Company, Ltd. The latter company's western manager, Mr. Max Schott, had persuaded them to form a syndicate to take up the so-called Leal option on a claim to molybdenum in Bartlett Mountain near Climax, Colorado. Mr. Leal was given cash. Mr. E. G. Heckendorf and his associates received 25% of the Climax shares issued upon Climax Molybdenum Company's incorporation.

The American Metal Company, Ltd., had been incorporated in 1887, but its thirty-some stockholders allowed it to operate more as a partnership. Some of the stock was owned in Germany and England. During World War I the Alien Property Custodian took over the German-held shares and later sold them at auction. The original stockholders regularly approved sharing about 33% of profits with directors and executives on a fixed basis of division. The directors and executives left these bonuses and other funds on deposit with the company as banker, drawing on their accounts for payment of business and personal bills. In speculative new mining ventures it was common practice for the management to take individual shares in the risk as well as to authorize corporate investment. This was the type of syndicate that formed Climax. The syndicate participants had their accounts charged with more than $1,000,000 before Climax began to operate profitably. No funds were secured through public financing.

Before 1916 molybdenum had been almost unknown to the general public in America, although European metallurgists had used it experimentally in alloy steels. At first the syndicate directed its endeavors toward developing the mining claim and a commercially practicable milling operation. The wartime scarcity of alloy metals created a temporary demand. This demand induced by the war, however, had vanished within a year after the mine and mill got into production. The directors and backers of the company hesitated to put up money for research, for they were then unconvinced that this was the key to profitable development. Finally, by trial and error Climax engineers worked out with automobile company metallurgists a satisfactory alloy that was approved by the Society of Automotive Engineers in 1925.

By 1930, the company's long struggle to gain acceptance for molybdenum steels demonstrated to directors the need for continuous aggressive research. Early aggressive selling had induced users to put too much molybdenum into the steel, which made the alloy brittle and hard to work. In 1931 Climax set up a research laboratory in Detroit under the operation of the wholly owned subsidiary Climax Molybdenum Company of Michigan, which worked with the automobile companies and other large users to develop scientific specifications for special uses of alloy steel and iron. Molybdenum in steel alloys counteracted fatigue and increased tensile strength. Also, molybdenum alloys proved advantageous for use under conditions of high temperature and pressure, severe stress, and vibration. In combination, molybdenum improved the effectiveness of certain other alloying metals. In cast iron it gave greater malleability and impact strength. Research also developed uses for molybdenum in colors, ceramics, and catalytic and other chemical processes. The amount of molybdenum sold for these latter uses was small, but they offered some diversification independent of the iron and steel industry.

In 1935 the board approved revaluation of the mine based on a thorough investigation by an independent engineer. The Hoskold Formula, an accepted method of mine valuation, was used for this purpose. An account was included on the balance sheet for Discovered Increment at $74,131,250, and offset by a Discovered Increment Surplus account of like amount. Both accounts were reduced annually for depletion. At the time of this revaluation, estimates were made that ore reserves contained 625,000,000 pounds of molybdenum, that is, a 50-year life with annual extraction at 12,500,000 pounds and annual net profits at $5,000,000.

The mine accounted for about 80% of world production before World War II. Smaller deposits owned by other companies were located principally in the United States, Canada, Latin America, Africa, Russia, and Norway. In 1939, the production of these other mines amounted to more than 10,000,000 pounds a year. Before the development of a market for molybdenum by Climax, world production had amounted to less than 700,000 pounds in any one year.

The method of mining at Climax consisted of underground caving. The mill at the mine ground the large chunks of ore into successively finer particles, from which molybdenum sulphide was concentrated by an oil flotation process. The ratio of recovery was about one ton of concentrate (80% to 90% fine) to 165 tons of ore. Before World War II the company shipped over half its molybdenum production abroad. The concentrate used domestically was sent to Langloth, Pennsylvania, in the Pittsburgh steel district. There, the wholly owned subsidiary Climax Molybdenum Company of Pennsylvania converted the concentrate into ferro-molybdenum, calcium molybdate, and other molybdenum products. These were sold principally to iron and steel producers for use in alloys.

The company's growth before World War II was indicated by the increase in sales from $1,463,000 in 1931 to $20,475,000 in 1939, the latest year for which sales figures were released. Net profits for those years increased from $109,000 to $10,-309,000. The 2,520,000 shares of common stock outstanding at the end of 1943 had a market value of about $88,000,000. Net working capital exceeded $16,000,000, and there was no funded debt. The first small dividend was declared in 1933, and dividends were paid consistently after that. Stock was listed on the New York Stock Exchange on September 8, 1937. The number of stockholders had increased from approximately 2,500 in that year to approximately 7,000 in 1944.

Top Management Organization — Directors and Executives

The board of directors as of December 31, 1943, was as shown in Exhibit 4, with the year first elected, the number of shares of stock owned directly or indirectly, and the principal affiliations of the directors.

EXHIBIT 4. CLIMAX MOLYBDENUM COMPANY: INFORMATION REGARDING DIRECTORS

Directors	*Year First Elected*	*Number of Shares Owned*
Otto Sussman, Chairman of the Board of Directors, The American Metal Company, Ltd.	1918	121,838
[The American Metal Company, Ltd., owned		225,000]
Harold K. Hochschild, President, The American Metal Company, Ltd.	1923	137,272
Bernard N. Zimmer, Vice President, The American Metal Company, Ltd.	1926	7,400
Max Schott, President, Climax Molybdenum Company	1926*	37,050
James B. Thorpe, Vice President, Climax Molybdenum Company	1936	3,500
Arthur B. Hyman, Lawyer, Member of Firm of Paskus, Gordon & Hyman	1944	1,280
Carl M. Loeb, Broker, Senior Partner, Carl M. Loeb, Rhoades & Co.	1918	none†

*Had served also in 1918-1919.
†There were large family holdings.

SOURCE: Proxy Statement, 1944.

This listing of stock owned does not include all closely related interests of directors or holdings of executives and employees of Climax Molybdenum Company and The American Metal Company, Ltd., which it is estimated represented over half the shares outstanding in November, 1944. Directors were paid a fee of $50 for each meeting attended. They held eight directorships in other companies.

The executive organization in outline was as follows: the president; a senior vice president; a vice president in charge of mining and production at Climax, Colorado; a vice president in charge of manufacturing at Langloth, Pennsylvania; and a vice president in charge of metallurgy, development, and field men, including the research laboratory in Detroit, Michigan. Other officers were the secretary, treasurer, and their assistants. All officers had their headquarters in New York, and the president's direct participation in activities knit the organization closely together. A Metallurgy Committee had recently been formed by the men in metallurgy and manufacturing to co-ordinate developments.

The directors had substantial interests in the company through their own holdings or the holdings of members of their families. Four of the seven directors had been active in the early days of Climax, and the board had continued to have a sense of direct responsibility. Directors sought reports on proposed expenditures from executives but made the ultimate decisions on the basis of what they believed the company should risk. Each director felt that he had ultimate responsibility, and therefore the group chose to consider questions as a board rather than through an executive committee. The board had a critical view toward diversification and new lines of expenditure; however, members recognized the possibility that they might discourage ideas by overdoing the critical approach and made an effort to encourage expression of ideas and reactions by executives. The president explained that the board invited executives not on the board to attend meetings, and it avoided taking part in operations, limiting its participation to forming policies and approving major expenditures.

Methods of Communication between Directors and Executives

The active executives were represented on the board by the president and senior vice president, but other members of the board had had experience in the company. Mr. Carl M. Loeb had been the first president. Mr. Otto Sussman served as president after the sudden death of Mr. Brainerd F. Phillipson in 1930 until Mr. Schott was elected in 1931. Mr. Bernard N. Zimmer formerly had been a vice president. Mr. Harold K. Hochschild was secretary and had been closely related to the development of Climax almost from the beginning. The law firm of which Mr. Arthur B. Hyman was a member handled litigation, involving a searching study of the company's history.

The board remained small, and all members were located in New York, where the company's main offices were. Because of the directors' background, telephone calls and brief informal meetings between directors and executives cleared many questions for which directors felt a sense of responsibility. On more weighty problems of policy, to be decided at board meetings, the executives prepared memoranda which the president sent to directors before their meetings.

Board Meetings and Minutes, and Problems Submitted to the Board

Although executives and directors worked out many questions informally, problems calling for board action were submitted at board meetings. Ordinarily directors were able to reach unanimous agreement on important issues after discussion. The following are indicative of the problems dealt with currently:

Construction of new mill. Vice president's memorandum of recommendation included in minutes.

Disbursements from employees' aid fund. Reported by president, and board renewed fund.

Agreements on patent rights.

Bond subscriptions.

Emergency war equipment. Memorandum included in minutes. New manufacturing process, memorandum previously sent to directors, copy in minutes.

Dividend declaration.

Legal authorization, such as replacing lost stock certificates for bank account signatures.

Operating and financial statistics and business conditions.

Regular meetings, which were held monthly, were well attended. Special meetings were called on occasion, for example, to consider the annual report to stockholders. Once a year a special committee of nonsalaried directors was formed to distribute the bonus fund.

Directors' Methods of Handling Problems

The illustrations in this section do not purport to cover the entire range of problems faced by directors in the history of Climax Molybdenum Company.

The first of these illustrations has to do with the original venture into the molybdenum business and the judgment exercised by the management of The American Metal Company, Ltd., in apportioning the ownership and business risks among the corporate and individual members of the syndicate. A minority stockholder of The American Metal Company, Ltd., on December 31, 1938, brought suit in the Supreme Court of New York against Climax Molybdenum Company and certain individuals, most of whom had been or currently were directors, officers, or employees of The American Metal Company, Ltd. The general grounds of the action were that the individual directors of the latter company had taken for themselves shares in the Climax venture that should have gone to The American Metal Company, Ltd., and therefore that the profits from Climax should be turned back to the latter company. The trial court had found in favor of the plaintiffs, but the Appellate Division unanimously reversed the lower court and completely acquitted the defendants.[1] The opinion of the Appellate Division stated in part:

[1] *Turner, et al.*, v. *The American Metal Company Ltd., et al.*, 50 N.Y.S. 2d 800 (1st Dept.) (1944). "This is a stockholders' derivative action instituted on behalf of The American Metal Company, Limited, a New York corporation (hereinafter referred to as 'American Metal'). It is a consolidation of two actions brought by stockholders owning 165 out of a total of over 1,200,000 shares of common stock. The earlier action was begun on December 31, 1938, by the holder of 100 shares acquired in that year, and the latter by a holder, since 1929, of 65 shares. Plaintiffs acquired their stock many years after the challenged occurrences. No claim was asserted by any one until over twenty years after the alleged wrongful acts. Parenthetically, it may be observed that recent legislation enacted while this appeal was pending now commands that in an action such as this 'it must be made to appear that plaintiff was a stockholder at the time of the transaction of which he complains or that his stock thereafter devolved upon him by operation of law'."

* * * * * *

"The complaint charges defendant directors with breach of their fiduciary obligation to American Metal in that (1) they wilfully and fraudulently took for themselves 90% of the interest of American Metal in a molybdenum enterprise, which interest was the property of American Metal, and (2) since 1918, in cooperation with defendant Climax, which had been organized in that year, (a) they wrongfully caused American Metal to put its funds, facilities, resources, personnel, credit and good-will at the disposal of Climax for the benefit of themselves and Climax and (b) they wrongfully caused American Metal to refrain from competing with Climax in the sale of molybdenum."

...In determining whether it was a valid exercise of business judgment for the directors of American Metal to allot 90% of Metal's interest in the molybdenum enterprise to individual participants and limit American Metal's interest to only 10% it becomes necessary to consider the situation as it presented itself to the management of American Metal when the challenged allotment was made....

...Berthold Hochschild [father of Harold K. Hochschild, one of the present Climax directors] who controlled the largest American holding of the company, who was its chief executive and whose decision was virtually final on questions of policy, looked upon the venture as a "war baby" and wished to discard it entirely. A factor which induced American Metal in August, 1917, to build the mill at Climax and to open up the mine had been the anticipated Russian demand for molybdenum. With the advent of the Russian Revolution early in November, 1917, that market collapsed. When it became obvious that the cost of the molybdenum project would be far in excess of the original estimates, that the anticipated Russian market was lost, that, at best, the molybdenum venture was speculative, the heads of American Metal had about decided that the Leal option should not be taken up and that the enterprise should be altogether abandoned. It was then that Berthold Hochschild's ultimatum came that, if the officers wished to go forward with the venture, they should assume 90% of the risk, with American Metal taking the balance. He insisted that, in view of the uncertainties, American Metal's participation should be a small one. Accordingly, the directors and officers of American Metal agreed that the option should be exercised, and that American Metal's interest in the venture should be 10% of the syndicate, i.e., $7\frac{1}{2}\%$ of the total venture.... [The Heckendorf interests were to get 25% of the stock in partial payment for the claim.]

* * * * *

The Climax venture, we think, was honestly considered a speculation and a risk by the directors of American Metal, and the limitation by them of American Metal's participation to $7\frac{1}{2}\%$, in the light of circumstances as they existed in the latter part of 1917, was not a breach of fiduciary duty but was a valid exercise of sound business judgment.

* * * * *

The determination of such a question of business policy lay with the board of directors. The power to determine exists even where the directors...might have a personal interest in the determination. The law is settled that while the dual position of directors makes the fair exercise of judgment by them more difficult and requires a court to scrutinize these transactions with care, it does not "alone suffice to render the transactions void."....As we find that the board acted honestly and in entire good faith, there may be no judicial interference with their judgment.

The concurrence of all five appellate judges in this opinion reversed the trial court, denied the claims made on behalf of The American Metal Company, Ltd., and cleared all individual defendants.

The appellate opinion reversing the trial court considered it significant that the original decision of the managing directors of The American Metal Company, Ltd., had been confirmed at a later board meeting. At this meeting the board included disinterested new members who had become directors through purchase of former German-held stock from the Alien Property Custodian.

> Shortly thereafter, a meeting of the board of directors was had, and...the holdings...were offered to American Metal in line with the intimation of the Alien Property Custodian.
> ...when this offer was presented [two new directors], who had not the slightest interest in Climax but who owned or represented very large interests in American Metal, were appointed by the board to serve on a committee to investigate and determine whether the offer should be accepted.
>
> * * * * *
>
> Its decision not to purchase the Climax stock from the participants we are persuaded was made in good faith and in the exercise of honest judgment....The internal affairs, questions of policy of management, and expediency of contracts of a corporation are subject to the control of a board of directors, and in so far as those directors are honest, capable and independent, their judgement is final.[1]

Another function of directors was the determination of executive compensation. The board set the president's salary, and nonexecutive directors formed a committee once a year to

[1] Ibid.

determine the amount and allocation of the bonus fund, as explained elsewhere.

When Mr. Phillipson, president of Climax, died in 1930, the board elected one of the directors, Mr. Otto Sussman, as president until a successor could be found. The directors were active in considering possible successors; they sought suggestions from a leading alloy steel metallurgist, and they considered men within the organization. The general manager was an engineer and the other key executives also were expert technical men. Although the board recognized the contribution that each of the key executives was making, the members believed none of these men had quite the type of business experience needed to maintain contact with their constantly growing European market. Mr. Schott, who had been close to Climax from the beginning, had been elected a director in 1926 and appointed a vice president in 1930. He had had responsible administrative experience in The American Metal Company, Ltd., and on September 11, 1931, the board elected him president of Climax.

The vice president formerly in charge of research retired in 1943, the vice president in charge of operations at Langloth, Pennsylvania, resigned in 1942, and other changes in executive personnel were occasioned by the drastic curtailment in normal foreign trade and adjustment to wartime production. The president discussed these changes with directors before taking action, and the board minutes included some of the termination arrangements.

Participation of directors in Climax affairs was further illustrated by their rejection of the proposal to establish a research laboratory in the 1920's. Mr. Phillipson had urged setting up such a laboratory for the study of molybdenum metallurgy at various times from 1920 to 1930, while he was president, but the directors had considered the outlook too hazardous to justify the expenditure. The syndicate had opened up the mine originally very largely as a speculation. The directors' business experience had been in the field of base metals, such as copper, lead, and zinc, which had an established world market. Promotion of molybdenum subsequently proved to need a distinctly different point of view; the company had to find and demonstrate uses. Not until 1930 did the board approve estab-

lishing a metallurgical laboratory in Detroit, which was dedi-
cated in 1931 with the motto, "MOLY ON ITS MERITS ONLY."

The method used in this company to draw the line between
the functions of directors and those of executives was developed
to avoid confusion in negotiation of contracts. Some directors
had continued to participate with the new president in contract
negotiations. It became apparent to them that the business had
expanded in volume and complexity to a point where this
participation tended to work at cross purposes. To clear up
relationships the board adopted the following resolution on
November 6, 1931.

> RESOLVED: That the President be, and he hereby is, author-
> ized to conclude with the Company's European agents a con-
> tract to expire not later than December 31, 1933, to cover the
> Company's selling arrangements in Europe, on such terms as
> he may consider advisable and in the best interests of the Com-
> pany, subject to the foregoing opinion of the Board in regard to
> the minimum terms to be stipulated by the Company in the
> event that he should negotiate such new selling arrangement
> on the basis of outright sale, instead of on joint account, and
> subject also to the abovementioned opinion of the Board regard-
> ing the maximum concession to be granted by the Company
> in regard to its guaranteed profit on the business.

In carrying out the functions as defined, the president was
careful to make comprehensive outlines, as occasion arose,
covering the company's policy in major fields, such as pricing,
labor relations, and maintenance of supply. The directors
studied these statements for background, discussed them for
clarification, and at times took formal action on them depend-
ing on the need for final authorization.

For instance, in March, 1939, the president prepared a review
of price policy. This review was studied by the directors, who
called for a supplementary report on certain aspects. The
theme of these reports had to do with policies adopted to over-
come the early resistance to molybdenum.

> In the early years (1917-1925) of Climax history, the alloy
> steel industry as a whole was not particularly interested in
> producing alloy steels containing molybdenum for the following
> reasons:

a. There was no assurance of a sufficient supply.
b. There was not sufficient knowledge based on commercial experience regarding the merits of molybdenum as an alloying element.
c. There was uncertainty as to price.

Progressive price cuts through 1932 had been made possible by economies of new procedures and assured supply. Subsequently, molybdenum prices had been held at 1932 levels, in spite of increases in steel prices. The president recommended and the board approved making no change in policy. Prices were competitive with other alloys, and minor changes would not materially affect the final cost of steel, since on an average there were only about five pounds of "moly" used to one ton of steel.

On December 28, 1939, the president wrote to stockholders, as authorized by the board, quoting in full a letter from the State Department concerning the so-called moral embargo on molybdenum. This letter quoted in full President Roosevelt's statement of December 2, 1939, and commented:

We understand that this request applies to Russia, Germany, and Japan. We have advised the Department of State that we shall be guided by our Government's policy. We have also informed the Department that we have contracts with customers in Germany but that, due to the American neutrality legislation and the Allied blockade, no shipments under these contracts have been made since the outbreak of the war.

During the past five years the proportion of our sales to the said countries to our total sales has been as follows:

Year	Per cent of Total
1935	52.97
1936	54.89
1937	53.02
1938	72.11
1939	57.80

The extent to which this request will affect your Company's business under present conditions depends on various factors the influence of which cannot now be foreseen. We understand that in certain foreign countries not affected by this situation the consumption of molybdenum in 1940 is expected to be materially greater than in 1939. Our domestic sales have shown an upward trend during the year 1939 both actually and in proportion to our total business.

In addressing our stockholders in this matter, we desire to correct any erroneous impressions that may have arisen. Molybdenum is widely used in alloy steels of high quality but it is added to such steels usually in small amounts, averaging between two-tenths and four-tenths of one per cent in the steel. It is safe to estimate that not more than one per cent of all the molybdenum consumed in the world during the past three years has gone into aircraft of all types — commercial and military.

The primary uses of molybdenum are for peace-time industrial purposes. Like many other commodities to which that statement applies, molybdenum can be considered a war material only to the extent that the entire industries of a country are geared to a war basis.

By Order of the Board of Directors,
MAX SCHOTT, President

During World War II the Climax laboratory, metallurgists, and engineers worked with the Office of Scientific Research and Development on problems of high priority. The president worked out with the board a policy for maintaining the secrecy of government projects while keeping the directors informed of potential financial commitments for which they had responsibility to stockholders. He reported that the board had left nothing undone to assure maximum utilization of the company's resources for the war effort.

Reports of Management to Stockholders

The board authorized the president's letter to stockholders each year to accompany the formal financial statements and auditors' certificate. The letter usually was a page long and regularly commented on earnings and dividends. Until World War II, it furnished data on sales and production. In addition, the letters in recent years outlined such topics as the decision to set up a self-insurance reserve against war risks, the restriction of foreign sales, the effect of this restriction on prospective sales and the increase of domestic sales, the capital expenditure program before and during the war, the beginning of gradual production curtailment, the death of a director, the settlement of a lawsuit, and the receipt of an Army-Navy "E" Award.

Part of the compensation of executives and employees was based on earnings and was determined by a committee of non-participating directors in accordance with the company's charter. The annual report for 1943 carried the following note on this subject, "Net Profit above shown is after deduction for additional compensation paid to officers and employees in accordance with the provisions of subdivision (k) of Article IX of the Certificate of Incorporation, in total of. . . $354,565." This amount was considerably less than the 5% of net profits authorized by the charter for distribution.

Recent annual meetings of stockholders have been attended by approximately 40 persons, most of whom already had given proxies to the management. The shares voted in recent years in proportion to the total were: 86.31%, 1942; 83.53%, 1943; 84.78%, 1944. Those attending included representatives of investment trusts and investment banking houses and other institutional investors as well as individuals. All discussions of operations, questions raised by stockholders, and replies were recorded verbatim, but no transcript was sent to stockholders.

CHAPTER VI

General Foods Corporation

General Foods Corporation is included in the study because it has had, since it was first listed in 1922, a board of inside and outside directors. In 1945, nine of the company's directors were outside men, one was the largest stockholder, and six were operating executives.

Mr. C. W. Post established the underlying business of General Foods Corporation in 1895. Before he died in 1914, he had turned the management over to a board of eight executives, whom he named as his executors. After his estate was settled, the company was reorganized for public issue of shares, and the stock listed on the New York Stock Exchange in 1922. The present name was adopted in 1929.

The original line of Postum Cereal, Post Toasties, and Instant Postum was expanded following the recapitalization in 1922 by the addition of a new cereal product, Post's Bran Flakes, and by the acquisition of established companies making a wide variety of nationally known grocery specialties. Purchases were made through exchanges of common stock. The following companies are a partial list of those merged: The Jell-O Company, Inc.; Igleheart Brothers; Minute Tapioca Company; Walter Baker & Company, Limited; Franklin Baker Company; The Log Cabin Products Company; Sanka Coffee Corporation; Cheek-Neal Coffee Corporation; La France Manufacturing Company; Calumet Baking Powder Company; Certo Corporation; Diamond Crystal Salt Company; General Foods Company; General Seafoods Corporation; North Atlantic Oyster Farms, Inc.; Bennett Day Importing Company; Atlantic Gelatine Company; Bireley's Inc.; Gaines Food Co., Inc.; Snider Packing Corporation; Ray-Maling Co., Inc.; and Jersey Cereal Company.

Expansion, however, was not limited to acquisition of well-established products. The company's Research Department was constantly developing new products. In addition, research had found new ways of using by-products, perfected methods of enriching flours, developed products for the military services, and developed substitutes for products unobtainable during the war.

One of the company's directors later recalled that during the period of rapid expansion, businessmen were talking in terms of horizontal or vertical integration. Someone described General Foods Corporation as "circular integration." This director, however, preferred to think of the integration as a funnel. He interpreted the over-all process of acquisition as being shaped by the methods of distributing grocery specialties. The guiding concept was "mass selling" and acquisition of companies that would fit together through the funneling of their products through common distribution channels.

Management had seen the advantages of mass production and predicated the expansion program on the application of this concept to selling. Early in the program the vision of mass selling was portrayed in a graphic volume outlining the prospective development. The individuality of the acquired lines was retained, and production continued in wholly owned subsidiaries or divisions under the functional supervision of the parent corporation, which put primary emphasis on the development of distribution through consolidating sales and advertising policies. Present sales organization methods were the culmination of continuous experiments.

Since the high seasonality of sales had made it difficult for the old Postum Cereal Company to maintain an efficient salesforce, finding complementary seasonal products was another of the factors bearing on the acquisition of additional companies.

No one in this early expansion period knew how many different products one salesman could efficiently handle. Consequently, when sales executives thought the number of products was becoming unwieldy for salesmen, they set up new distributing groups.

Each of these distributing groups had institutional, wholesale, and retail salesforces. The first two salesforces took direct orders from institutions and wholesalers; the retail force was made up of missionary salesmen only.

By 1928-1929, there were three distributing groups for the packaged goods line: (1) Post Products Company, Inc., which sold, in addition to the products of the former Postum Company, those of the Jell-O, Igleheart Brothers, and Minute Tapioca companies; (2) Baker Associated Companies, Inc., which sold Walter Baker chocolates and cocoas, Franklin Baker coconut, Maxwell House coffees and teas, and Log Cabin syrup; and (3) Calumet-Certo Company, Inc., which sold the baking powder and pectin products of those names and the products of La France Manufacturing Company. There was also a distributing group which dealt with somewhat different problems.

The sales executives constantly educated division managers in the executive point of view and the new mass selling objectives. These men in turn selected and educated district managers. Meanwhile, the sales organization conducted local experiments to find out how one group could handle the entire line.

Eventually all the packaged grocery specialties were brought together under one organization directed by the vice president in charge of sales, who also was president of the wholly owned subsidiary, General Foods Sales Company, Inc. The semi-perishable grocery product lines developed after purchase of the quick-freezing process were separately distributed through the wholly owned subsidiary, Birds Eye-Snider, Inc. (formerly Frosted Foods Sales Corporation). Efficient mass production of some key items in the main line of grocery specialties had resulted in production of joint products for which different methods of distribution were required.

Sales, which in 1922 were $17,800,000 annually, increased to over $295,000,000 in 1944. Common shares outstanding on December 31, 1944, totaled 5,575,463, with a balance sheet value of $94,167,534. Dividends were paid consistently, and the number of shareholders had increased to about 68,000. Preferred stock, which had a balance sheet value of $15,000,000, was called in December, 1944, and redeemed as of January 31, 1945. On February 1, 1945, $25,000,000 was borrowed by the issuance of unsecured notes.

Top Management Organization — Directors and Executives

The directors with the number of shares beneficially owned were listed as shown in Exhibit 5 in the March 9, 1945, Proxy Statement.

EXHIBIT 5. GENERAL FOODS CORPORATION: INFORMATION REGARDING DIRECTORS

	Principal Occupation or Employment	*Year First Elected Director*	*Shares of Common Stock Beneficially Owned, February 15, 1945*
Daniel M. Beach	Lawyer; member of the firm of Harris, Beach, Keating, Wilcox and Dale, Rochester, N. Y.	1925	1,000
Robert S. Cheek	Retired; one of the owners of the Maxwell House Coffee business at time of acquisition by the Company	1928	12,000
S. Sloan Colt	Banker; President of Bankers Trust Company, New York City	1932	100*
Marjorie Post Davies	Daughter of C. W. Post, founder of original predecessor of the Company	1936	281,325
William S. Gray, Jr.	Banker; President of Central Hanover Bank & Trust Company, New York City	1935	100*
Robert Lehman	Investment banker; member of the firm of Lehman Brothers, New York City	1930	100*
Charles W. Littlefield	Lawyer; member of the firm of Littlefield & Marshall, New York City	1938	1,200
Carl J. Schmidlapp	Banker; Vice President of The Chase National Bank of the City of New York	1922	500*
Sidney J. Weinberg	Investment banker; member of the firm of Goldman, Sachs & Co., New York City	1930	100*
Ernest L. Woodward	Farmer; one of the owners of the Jell-O business at time of acquisition by the Company in 1925	1942†	33,400
Colby M. Chester	Chairman of the Executive Committee	1922	20,075
Clarence Francis	Chairman of the Board	1932	4,040
Austin S. Igleheart	President	1926	200*
Charles W. Metcalf	Executive Vice President	1934	4,600
John S. Prescott	Vice President, Secretary, and General Counsel	1923	232*
Udell C. Young	Vice President	1937	100

*Excluding contingent interests.
†Previously director, 1925-1928.

SOURCE: Proxy Statement, 1945.

Directors were paid a fee of $50 for each meeting attended. They owned about 7% of the stock. Directors, including executive-directors, held a total of 107 other directorships in banks, trust companies, insurance companies, railroads, utilities, and industrial and mercantile companies (approximately 50 in the latter two groups).

Before an executive accepted an invitation to go on another board, it was customary for him to discuss the question informally with board members, and he was guided by their reaction. The board believed that if General Foods Corporation was to have the advantage of outside directors, it in turn must allow and encourage executives to act as directors in appropriate companies.

When there was a vacancy or an expected vacancy on the board, top executives and the Executive Committee, which was made up of both executives and directors, discussed possible candidates. They tried to start discussion far enough in advance so they could observe the candidates before final selection. In practice, the executives nominated candidates to the board, but only after the directors had had an opportunity to approve the choice. The management submitted names of nominees to the stockholders in the annual statement soliciting proxies. Stock ownership, according to one director, in itself was not an adequate qualification for a director. One had to feel some obligation for public service and a sense of trusteeship. To make a good director a man had to have the fundamental qualifications of character, ability, and breadth of viewpoint, including a sense of business ethics and public responsibility, plus long-range foresight as distinguished from dependence on expediency. Directors agreed that a cohesive group and the spirit pervading it were more important than a count of votes. Many qualified men had come into General Foods Corporation through the mergers, but their number was so large it was obviously impossible to add them all to the board.

Through the years the practice had arisen of having more than half the membership made up of outside men, and the remainder, senior executives. The primary objective, however, was to get the most capable men available regardless of this general proportion.

There were a number of management committees set up in the company to facilitate the work of directors and executives. The Executive Committee had power to act for the board and met monthly between board meetings. The committee frequently invited a "roving" member of the board to meetings in addition to the regular members. The chairman appointed and the board approved nonexecutive directors to compose the Salary and the Auditing Committees. The Salary Committee had the responsibility of reviewing and approving executive compensation. The Auditing Committee, of nonexecutive directors, had the responsibility of selecting the independent public accountants employed and of working out with them the scope of the audit in relation to internal controls. The Accounting Review Committee of outside directors was responsible for studying the complete audit report, which was addressed to the board of directors, and conferring with the auditors about any questions or suggestions. The board also created a temporary committee of directors for the sale of fixed assets. Another special committee was appointed to determine policy for joining trade and charitable organizations and making contributions.

The Executive Council, composed of 13 senior executives, held regular weekly meetings presided over by the president. The objectives of the council were to help coordinate the various branches of the company, to develop executive teamwork, to bring about discussion of problems of interest to all departments, and to iron out major interdepartmental differences.

The Management Committee, which was made up of 50 or more supervisory employees, was the outgrowth of a former Operating Committee. It met quarterly and was found a useful means of keeping the key supervisory staff informed of quarterly results, current operations, and objectives.

The following description of the administrative organization was given in an office memorandum of December 14, 1943.

The organization for corporate administration is made up of three major groups: (1) Executive — composed of the chairman, who is the chief executive officer; the president, who is the chief coordinating officer; and the executive vice president, who is the chief operating officer and is in charge of adminis-

EXHIBIT 6. GENERAL FOODS CORPORATION
Condensed Organization Chart as of December 14, 1945

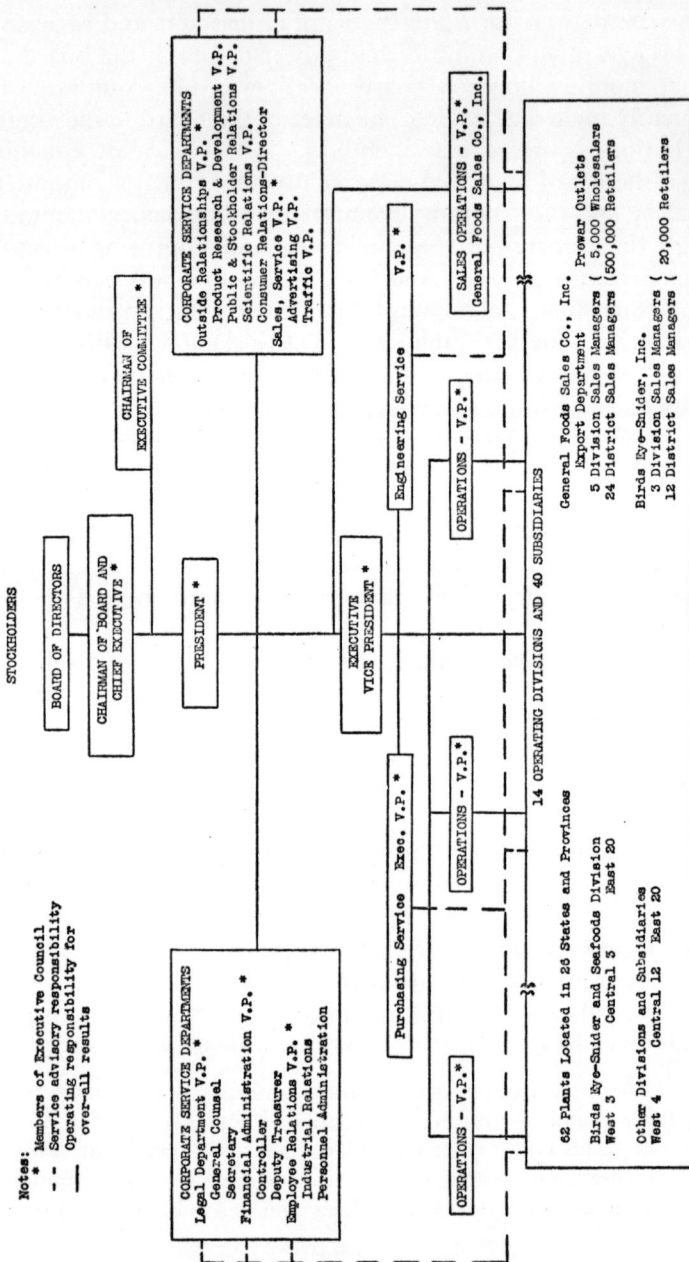

STOCKHOLDERS

BOARD OF DIRECTORS

CHAIRMAN OF BOARD AND
CHIEF EXECUTIVE *

CHAIRMAN OF
EXECUTIVE COMMITTEE *

PRESIDENT *

EXECUTIVE
VICE PRESIDENT *

CORPORATE SERVICE DEPARTMENTS
Outside Relationships V.P. *
Product Research & Development V.P.
Public & Stockholder Relations V.P.
Scientific Relations V.P.
Consumer Relations-Director
Sales, Service V.P. *
Advertising V.P.
Traffic V.P.

CORPORATE SERVICE DEPARTMENTS
Legal Department V.P. *
General Counsel
Secretary
Financial Administration V.P. *
Controller
Deputy Treasurer
Employee Relations V.P. *
Industrial Relations
Personnel Administration

Purchasing Service Exec. V.P. *

Engineering Service   V.P. *

SALES OPERATIONS - V.P. *
General Foods Sales Co., Inc.

OPERATIONS - V.P. *

OPERATIONS - V.P. *

OPERATIONS - V.P. *

OPERATIONS - V.P. *

14 OPERATING DIVISIONS AND 40 SUBSIDIARIES

General Foods Sales Co., Inc.
   Export Department   Prewar Outlets
   5 Division Sales Managers (5,000 Wholesalers
   24 District Sales Managers (500,000 Retailers

Birds Eye-Snider, Inc.
   3 Division Sales Managers (20,000 Retailers
   12 District Sales Managers (

62 Plants Located in 26 States and Provinces

Birds Eye-Snider and Seafoods Division
   West 3   Central 5   East 20

Other Divisions and Subsidiaries
   West 4   Central 12   East 20

Notes:
  *   Members of Executive Council
  - - Service advisory responsibility
  —— Operating responsibility for
      over-all results

trative functions in the president's absence; (2) Operations —
composed of operating divisions and subsidiaries, wholly or
partially self-contained, through which the profits of the business
are derived and which are under the direction of corporate
vice presidents in charge of operations; and (3) Services —
which are composed of specialized functions essential to the
over-all administration of the corporation. They are under the
direction of corporate vice presidents.

The abbreviated organization chart, Exhibit 6, indicates the
functional organization and chief executive responsibilities.

Chairman of the Board and Chief Executive

The chairman of the board of this company also was the
chief executive, as indicated above. These were in reality
two separate groups of functions for which he had responsibility. He considered that his duties as chairman included
such responsibilities as representing the stockholders' point of
view; directing the board's discussions to policy formation in
distinction to operating techniques; following up board decisions to see that action resulted; informing the board of executive decisions and action; bringing executives and subsidiary
officers to board meetings; acting as prime mover in filling vacancies on the board; and performing the usual duties of chairman, such as officiating at meetings and appointing committees.

Methods of Communication between Directors and Executives

The preceding section covering the functions of the chairman indicates that he had taken the problem of getting information to the board as one of his definite duties. There was, in
addition, a sense of responsibility on the part of all the executives who were directors to bring before the board problems
which executives were considering and on which the other
directors might have questions or helpful points of view. Often
they raised these problems at informal luncheons or made
telephone calls about specific questions. One example of a
question informally discussed was foreign exchange problems
arising out of purchases of raw materials and foreign sales.
This informal relation between directors and executives was
fostered by social activities.

[75]

Other executives also had an opportunity of meeting the directors. Frequently at board meetings the head of a subsidiary or department reported on the work under his direction. Directors thus could become acquainted with key operating personnel.

Directors also contributed to the thought given to maintaining communication between the board and executives. After the Federal Securities Act and court decisions in 1933 had emphasized the liabilities of directors, one director prepared for discussion an eleven-point code of procedure for executives to follow to inform directors and consult with them on broad policies they were to pursue. This plan was his concept of how directors could get the information they needed in order to exercise the reasonable care of a prudent man without interfering with the executives in the ordinary and administrative business of the corporation. Several directors credited the frankness and openness of executives and directors with the high degree of respect and confidence prevailing between the board and the executives. In the informal contacts between directors and executives no special routine was observed. Ordinarily, however, a director would talk to the senior executive before taking up a question with a subordinate.

Beginning in March, 1931, the chairman of the board regularly prepared a memorandum covering a large number of the topics that the executives had been considering during the course of the month, and gave copies of this report to directors at the board meeting. Previously, the chairman or other executives had from time to time submitted memoranda on various projects to the board for the directors information. The effect of the regular reports which began in 1931 was to give the directors background for deciding on questions subsequently presented to them for formal consideration. These regular reports also gave directors assurance, in the opinion of one member, that they knew what action was being taken by executives on important issues.

The chairman prepared this report to the board by selecting from the notes kept by the secretary of the Executive Council items which had reached a stage which he thought would be of interest to the directors. He added to these items others that also might be of interest but had not come before the Executive Council. The chairman would call to the specific attention of the board any item of far-reaching effect when he asked for the directors' approval of the minutes, which included the report. Typically, these reports covered about six or eight pages and included topics such as the following: proposed form of annual report to stockholders, a plan to get stockholders' help as consumers, explanation of operations and earnings in subsidiaries, expense of promoting new products, inventory in hands of dealers, legal developments, research results, results of promotion plans, relations with customers, development of chain store outlets, advertising budgets, and perplexities facing management on account of price pressure. The chairman reported failures as well as favorable results.

The reports also generally carried a brief comment about major products or materials in which there had been developments affecting the course of business. The reports also carried executive decisions, such as the one to give a war bond bonus to employees in the service; arrangement of a special retirement plan for units not covered in the regular plan; receiving the "A" award for war food processes; and formation of policies on contributions and memberships as outlined by the committee for this purpose, copies of which were available to directors on request.

In addition, the chairman referred to letters received from servicemen concerning their old jobs, a film prepared for the employees' information on the company's retirement plan, and the report on special retirement payments. Recent reports nearly always had a paragraph on such topics as industrial relations, progress of negotiations with unions, and employee elections. Executive personnel changes also were reported through this medium.

The chairman's report for December 15, 1943, included reference to the new organization chart, which appears here as Exhibit 6.

In addition to these reports the chairman of the board prepared copies of agenda for each director to have for the monthly board meetings. The agenda, supported by copies of reports, minutes, and other data, had four sections:

1. Specific issues which the executives considered necessary for board discussion and action.
2. Issues previously discussed and acted on by the Executive Committee and presented for approval. These were reported to the board in minutes of the Executive Committee and frequently were discussed further before confirmation by the board.
3. Report of the chairman on executive action and developments of general interest. This report was officially a part of the minutes of the board, although normally the board took no specific action on individual items. Items were there, however, for board attention, should any member consider the issues ones on which the board should take more deliberate action.
4. Financial statistics by divisions as well as in total. These often were supplemented by comprehensive reports in person by presidents of subsidiaries or other key executives.

Board and Executive Committee Meetings and Minutes

The board of directors met monthly, and in addition, nonexecutive directors formed one-half or more of the Executive Committee, which the board considered primarily as an interim agency to act between board meetings. The committee's minutes were read, discussed, and approved at the following board meeting.

The following subjects are examples of those acted on or considered by the Executive Committee and reported in the minutes, which were subsequently submitted to the board for approval: sale of stock in a subsidiary, erecting a service building, borrowing from banks, CPA and proxy statements, the presence of CPA representative at annual stockholders' meeting, appointment of Profit Incentive Committee of nonexecutive directors, leases, inventory position, bonding of employees, changing the fiscal year, standard practices in industrial relations [a three-year review], investment policy, a comprehensive study of frosted foods activities and financial standing, proposed capital expenditures, plant visits preparatory to considering long-term investment program, report of Auditing Committee of directors on program for maintaining contact with the company's accounting staff and independent auditors, authorized limits for proposed sale of capital assets, progress of negotiation in strike, guaranty of subsidiary's contract, statement of policy on future purchases [at request of an executive], report of changes in radio program, extension of product into new markets, estimated operating cost during promotion of new product, report of reorganization of the Operating Committee.

Executives frequently took to the Executive Committee, through the chairman, issues on which they wished to get the reaction of directors but which had not been crystallized into a form for final decision.

Problems Submitted to the Board of Directors

The following much abbreviated items indicate, in a very general way and for one meeting only, the problems submitted to the board and the action it took on them. The items are grouped according to the method used by the chairman in preparing his agenda. All these items were considered to be included in the official minutes of the board.

1. The board received the controller's certificate of surplus and undivided profits, declared a common stock dividend, discussed and passed a resolution authorizing officers to renegotiate a government contract, appointed an assistant controller, authorized bank account signatures, and approved the minutes of the Executive Committee as recorded.
2. The board discussed and approved the minutes of the preceding Executive Committee meeting covering action on financial statements for the year 1943; forecast of cash requirements for the year 1944, including the time and probability of borrowing needs as explained by the treasurer; the basis of renegotiation; contributions to charity; detailed memorandum and personal presentation of capital expenditure program for an important subsidiary; War Loan subscription; and report on commodity position.
3. The report of the chairman attached to and approved as part of the minutes included a brief description of the following topics [six pages]:

    Sales and earnings, extra compensation, cash, inventories, dividends, outlook for sugar, outlook for cartons, and a detailed report on administrative reorganization of a specific division. This report described the former divisions and subsidiaries that were being brought together in this new division. The choice of name was explained and the problems of coordinating production, research, accounting, sales, and traffic administration. The report continued with the responsible executive's statement listing subsidiary officers and their responsibilities. Details were given to explain the organization of the sales department into divisions, districts, and branches, with the responsibilities that managers for these units were to have for trade and customer relations, sales, product merchandising, and local personnel administration, plus a list of products to be handled. The report about this new division concluded with an estimate of the proposed capital expenditure and prospective sales.

The chairman's report also explained findings of a stockholders' survey mailed with the dividend checks. The survey had covered stockholders' reaction to the annual report, research, dividend policy, directors' remuneration, minutes of annual meeting, selection of outside auditors, and the General Foods retirement plan.

The chairman's report also included personnel policy and a report on supervisors' meetings at which sales, production, and progress were discussed, and mentioned executive discussions on the status of the company, executive responsibilities, and the outlook for the new year, which had been explained at a tea party for the headquarters staff and parties in other plants. The chairman explained the course of action being followed in labor relations at three subsidiary plants where union negotiations were under way, including maintenance of membership order by the WLB in one plant.

The report also covered company policy toward employees in the armed forces.

4. Included for the board's information were the following financial statistics: the balance sheet, the earned surplus account, schedules of the trend of case sales, cash, and a detailed report of capital expenditures, showing the current year's authorizations with expenditures to date and prior year authorization balances with the current year's expenditures to date.

Listing these items fails to portray the atmosphere of mutual regard and inquiry that executives and directors considered characteristic features of board meetings. Not only did executives respect the character, ability, and caliber of the directors, but also, as one executive said, "We feel that these men appreciate our job, too, and the importance of our freedom to meet daily administrative affairs." As a result, this executive considered the board to be a stabilizing influence. Executives recognized that the questions directors asked about matters presented to them had great psychological weight in the initial analysis of an issue. They wanted to continue to be so well fortified with reasoned answers to anticipated questions that the board would never turn down an executive recommendation. The chief executive observed that this careful preparation for board meetings carried down in spirit to other levels of deliberation.

Directors' Methods of Handling Problems

The following selected illustrations indicate the methods used by the board to avoid occasions of self-dealing and, as trustees, to weigh judiciously the interests of stockholders, employees, and the public. These selections are simplified and taken from their context and do not portray the human interactions.

It was current policy for the Salary Committee, made up of outside directors, to set the salaries of the senior executives. In recent years, the executives who also were directors had withdrawn from the company's incentive compensation plan to avoid any criticism of profiting by their dual position of directors and executives. The directors' Auditing Committee selected independent outside auditors and received their detailed report.

Another illustration of the way potential conflicts of interest were handled is indicated in the following excerpt from the minutes of the Executive Committee, May 15, 1939:

> *Payment and Indemnification of Directors*...discussed and referred to the Advisory Committee [now Executive Council] for study, particularly the question of public policy involved in the subject of indemnification.

Also, when outside directors were elected or when executives were elected to other directorships, occasions arose when they might be called upon to act in a dual capacity. The directors and executives in General Foods Corporation were aware of this possibility and took steps to avoid embarrassment to individuals, as illustrated by the chairman's description of the development and choice of the refinancing plan announced in the latter part of 1944. During the year, various executives in the Executive Council meetings raised questions about future capital requirements, as they were planning work in their divisions. The tax department also had under consideration the relative disadvantage of preferred stock financing compared with bonds under current tax laws. During the course of the summer the executives began to formulate from these various discussions a broad, long-range program for meeting capital requirements. As this program began to take shape, it was discussed with individual directors and eventually in the Executive Committee. Directors agreed with the executives on the general need for funds and the advisability of taking action.

While this was being discussed, the board invited a disinterested nonexecutive director to serve with the Executive Committee in place of the commercial and investment bankers. Full advantage was taken of the technical knowledge that these directors had, but they were not in the position of participating in corporate action. Each of them, as well as representatives of other financial institutions, had the opportunity of presenting alternative plans to the Executive Committee. In due course the committee concluded that a preponderance of data pointed to a program which they then recommended to the full board of directors. The chairman explained that the directors having personal interest in the plan did not vote at the meeting when the plan was formally adopted.

On December 22, 1944, the chairman of the board and president wrote to common stockholders explaining the refinancing program and giving an abbreviated balance sheet showing the estimated effect of the refinancing. Excerpts from the letter follow:

> ...the board of directors has approved contracts, providing for the borrowing on February 1, 1945, of $25,000,000 on unsecured notes.

Of the proceeds, $16,293,750 will be used to finance the redemption on or about January 31, 1945, of the outstanding $15,000,000 par value 4½% Preferred Stock, at the specified redemption price of $107.50 per share, plus a sum in lieu of dividend to the redemption date. The balance of $8,706,250 less the incidental expenses connected with the financing, estimated not to exceed $20,000, will be added to the funds of the corporation.

The obligations to be issued are:

$5,000,000 2% serial notes, maturing $500,000 each six months from August 1, 1950, to February 1, 1955, both inclusive. These funds will be borrowed from Bankers Trust Company, Central Hanover Bank and Trust Company, and The Chase National Bank, all of New York.

$20,000,000 2¾% notes, maturing February 1, 1965. The corporation agrees to pay $500,000 each six months beginning August 1, 1955. Furthermore, the corporation may, if it so elects, pay an additional $500,000 each six months beginning August 1, 1950. These funds will be borrowed from the Metropolitan Life Insurance Company of New York.

In addition to the above provisions for periodic payments, both series of notes contain other provisions permitting payment in whole or in part.

The present revolving bank credit with the three banking institutions mentioned above, under which the corporation has the option to borrow up to $10,000,000 until February 1, 1947, is being canceled, and the annual charge under this arrangement will be eliminated.

* * * * *

The maximum interest charges on the $25,000,000 of notes will be $650,000 annually, compared with dividends of $675,000 on the $15,000,000 of preferred stock which is to be retired. Furthermore, under present tax laws, the interest payments are deductible by the corporation in arriving at income subject to income and profit taxes, whereas the preferred dividends are not.

With reorganization of the company following the settlement of Mr. Post's estate, the principal stockholders elected to the board of directors a group of outside businessmen including representatives of the underwriters of the public stock issues.

These new directors were instrumental in bringing in new executives and developing the comprehensive plan the company followed in expanding its line of products through acquisition of producing companies and introducing new lines.

In the summer of 1922, the company introduced Post's Bran Flakes, and the new product achieved remarkable popularity in just a few months. According to one director, the salesforce and broker representatives demonstrated that this additional product could be handled "in stride." He considered that the knowledge gained from that experience had much to do with the development of thinking along the lines which came to fruition in the expansion program starting with acquisition of the Jell-O Company in the latter part of 1925.

As one director reviewed the company's history, he felt that as executives had developed methods for assimilating other companies, the initial impetus in the setting of objectives, selection of executive personnel, and planning acquisitions tended to shift from directors to executives. An example of this shift in initiative was given by another director, who described the recent acquisition of Gaines Food Co., Inc. General Foods' operating executives had known for a long time that their subsidiaries were selling by-products to manufacturers of dog foods. The Executive Council at numerous meetings discussed the possibility of adding a line of dog food products. Members of various operating departments also studied this issue and the question became: Would it be better to develop a new line of dog food products or to purchase a well-established company in this field? The chief problem no longer was considered primarily as financial, as would have been the case in the early history of the company, but it involved complicated pension problems, labor problems, costs of brand development, and many similar issues. The Executive Council decided that it would be advantageous to acquire Gaines Food Co., Inc., and submitted this recommendation to the Executive Committee, which presented it to the board of directors for final approval.

This procedure followed the general policy previously confirmed by the board after careful deliberation, and made part of the minutes of the Executive Committee meeting on March 4, 1943, approved by the board of directors:

Acquisition Policy...The possibilities of such acquisitions should be explored provided the management was satisfied such purchases could be fitted into the organization without undue extension of executive attention and effort.

As the acquisition policy became established, the attention of the board, according to one director, shifted from problems of acquiring new companies to questions of product development; pricing; and public, labor, and governmental relations. For example, the board, as well as the Executive Committee, considered at length the procedure for executives to follow in dealing with the closed shop issue. A booklet had been issued to new employees for some years, which stated that employees had free right to collective bargaining, but that no one need join or refrain from joining any organization in order to be employed by the company. The minutes of the Executive Committee, March 14, 1939, approved by the board of directors, concluded:

It was agreed that the board of directors should be consulted in the event any closed shop issue became acute on broad questions of policy; details of labor relations to be handled by the management [executives].

Reports of Management to Stockholders

The management stated that careful attention was given to questions from stockholders and various means were used to keep stockholders informed of developments. The management sent letters about unusual events, such as the refinancing and redemption of the preferred stock issue and the formal adoption of the administrative organization plan. The proxy statement was sent as required by law.

The annual financial statement for several years had been expanded, according to one director, to give stockholders a feeling for the business as well as an objective statement of financial facts. For instance, the annual report for 1943 began with a five-year statistical summary of General Foods operations. This was followed by a discussion of the topic "Food *does fight* for Freedom," amplified by pictures, charts, and diagrams covering subjects under the following headings: Stockholders, Sales, Taxes, Earnings, Dividends, Assets, Inventories, Birds Eye, Plants, The "Bad News," Acquisitions, Research, Future Planning, Administration, Industrial Relations, Consumer Service, Advertising, Government Relations, The Outlook. Following this section there were pictorial analyses of the financial statements and a two-year financial comparison, supplemented with a table of sales, net profits, and dividends from 1922 to 1943. In addition to the usual listing of directors and officers, the report gave a list of principal plants and subsidiaries with the chief operating executives, sales officers, and division and district managers.

As was customary, at the annual meeting in 1944 the management welcomed stockholders' questions and opened for inspection the minutes of the board and Executive Committee meetings.

CHAPTER VII

Standard Oil Company (New Jersey)

The Standard Oil Company (New Jersey), because of its long history and great size, faces many problems of extreme importance in any study of directors which are not shown clearly in smaller companies or companies with less complicated ramifications. Moreover, its policy of having full-time directors with carefully defined duties illustrates one distinctive type of organization of boards of directors.

Standard Oil Company (New Jersey) was incorporated in 1882 and in 1911 was divested of its holdings in 33 other companies in the dissolution of the so-called oil trust. The Standard Oil Company (New Jersey) continued as an operating and holding company until 1927, when it transferred all operations to subsidiaries. After July 1, 1944, the parent company operated the marine transportation department. Jersey[1] was one of the largest corporate systems in the oil industry, with consolidated balance sheet assets, including 100 subsidiaries, of $2,328,000,000 at the end of 1943. This balance sheet also showed minority interests at book values approximating $250,-000,000. The consolidated group had over 90,000 employees. The parent company had over 149,000 stockholders, and there were 27,283,587 shares of stock outstanding. Dividends had been paid consistently since incorporation.

These statistics together suggest an almost incomprehensible complexity and multiplicity of management problems, even a cursory survey of which is beyond the scope of this paper. The following paragraphs, however, illustrate part of the context in which Jersey directors functioned. They dealt with oil production, transportation, refining, and marketing with the

[1]Throughout the case Jersey is used to refer either to the parent company Standard Oil Company (New Jersey) or the parent company and its subsidiaries, as the context makes clear.

[87]

implied problems of management as well as questions of domestic and international public policy. A brief historical background precedes the description of these problems.

In the same year in which the Standard Oil trust was formed, 1882, the trustees incorporated the Standard Oil Company of New Jersey as one of a number of operating companies. State and federal investigations and law suits against the trustees subsequently led them to transfer the holdings of all their properties to the Jersey company in 1892, at which time its name became Standard Oil Company. The "muckraking" investigations followed. Henry D. Lloyd's *Wealth against Commonwealth* was published in 1894, and Ida M. Tarbell's series of articles in *McClure's Magazine* was followed by the publication of her two-volume *The History of the Standard Oil Company* in 1904. This period was followed by a series of federal suits against the trusts, including the Standard Oil Company (New Jersey), and the decrees leading to their dissolution in 1911-1912. John D. Rockefeller retired from the management at this time. He and the large stockholders associated ·with him left the management in the hands of active executives. The properties left to Standard Oil Company (New Jersey) were primarily refining and marketing. When it was divested of its 33 units in 1911, kerosene for lamps and fuel oil were still the backbone of the business. Development of the automobile and incandescent light was just beginning.

Since the company had few producing properties, its major problem then and later was to find oil. This search was stimulated by the First World War.

At the beginning of World War II the petroleum industry's knowledge of oil occurrence had led experts to believe that over 40% of the land surface of the world might justify commercial exploration. The total proved reserves in the United States before World War II were thought to equal about 20 years' normal production. While further search was planned in the United States, this country had been far more intensively explored than elsewhere.

The two most promising oil fields, according to one director,[1]

---

[1]Wallace E. Pratt, *Oil in the Earth* (Lawrence, University of Kansas Press, 1942), p. 33.

were, first, the area around the Black, Caspian, and Red Seas, the Persian Gulf, and the eastern end of the Mediterranean Sea: the oil fields of Russia, Iran, Iraq, Arabia, Romania, and Egypt. The next most promising area was around the Gulf of Mexico and the Caribbean Sea: the oil fields of Venezuela, Colombia, Mexico, and the Gulf coast of the United States. Jersey had acquired reserves in both these general areas, but predominantly in the latter.

In the opinion of the same director, the restricting factor in oil extraction had become the man-made barriers to the free flow of oil: "Wars, embargoes, policies of national self-containment, cartels, exchange restrictions, tariffs and other trade barriers...."[1] For instance, in 1937-1938 Jersey's properties in Bolivia and Mexico had been expropriated. He was convinced that there was no longer fear of exhausting the supplies of oil in the earth. New methods for exploration had eliminated many of the former technical uncertainties.

Jersey production in 1943 was at the rate of 347,700 barrels a day in the United States, and 349,580 barrels a day in foreign fields, mainly Venezuela. The foreign production figures do not include output from the company's properties held by Germany and Japan.

Jersey expanded its transportation facilities to support the large proportion of its foreign production. Before World War II, it had a fleet of more than 200 tankers, the largest privately owned fleet in the world. Jersey's transportation facilities also included more than 3,000 miles of trunk pipe lines and 2,500 miles of gathering pipelines. The United States Government had taken control of transportation during the war, and called upon Jersey to supervise the government's construction program for approximately 500 tankers.

The Jersey management also was confronted with questions related to refining processes. In 1943 Jersey's domestic refineries ran 467,190 barrels a day and its foreign refineries, 407,392 barrels a day. Not only was refining conducted on a large scale, but questions of public policy arose because of the location of the refineries. Furthermore, basic changes were taking place in refinery processes. Products from petroleum,

[1]Ibid., p. 91.

particularly for military use, were recognized as complex chemical mixtures of hydrocarbons. These could be synthesized from crude oil fractions by careful, coordinated control of temperatures, pressures, and catalytic action in a variety of newly developed, highly technical refining processes: such as catalytic cracking, alkylation, isomerization, and hydrogenation. These cracking processes produced high octane gasoline. They also produced raw materials used in synthetic toluene for TNT. Another product produced was butadiene used in making synthetic rubber. Jersey refineries, according to the 1943 annual report to stockholders, supplied one-fourth of all 100-octane aviation gasoline produced for the Allies, and processes developed by Jersey had made more than enough toluene for all current TNT requirements of the armed services. Jersey's research program, which had been enlarged during the war, cost $6,500,000 in 1943. In that year, furthermore, Jersey spent $42,000,000 for manufacturing facilities, while it had spent $76,000,000 in 1942, and an average of $30,500,000 for the preceding five years. These figures did not include $62,-833,000 of government expenditures supervised by Jersey executives.

Even before the United States entered the war, Jersey was confronted with complex marketing problems because of its world-wide organization. Marketing organizations were maintained in the United Kingdom and in Europe, principally in France, the Scandinavian countries, Germany, Romania, and Italy. Also, in the Far East Jersey had a 50% interest in Standard-Vacuum Oil Company, which owned marketing, refining, and production facilities. In Latin America, it owned marketing outlets as well as large producing facilities. Its principal marketing areas in the United States were along the eastern seaboard. Since all these marketing areas were dependent in large measure on marine transportation, curtailment of this means of transportation upon the outbreak of war, as well as direct marketing restrictions, made drastic adjustments necessary.

Relations with government agencies became increasingly important during the war. The Petroleum Administrator for War, Office of Economic Affairs in the State Department,

Office of Price Administration, Office of Defense Transportation, War Shipping Administration, War Production Board, Interstate Commerce Commission, and Federal Power Commission, to mention only the most immediate domestic regulatory bodies, had to be considered in current operations. Even before the war, however, the petroleum industry had become one of public interest. Oil producing states had plans and agencies for conservation and proration. The Interstate Oil Compact and the Connally "Hot Oil" Act were designed to assist the states in their work.

Jersey's postwar problems depend in large measure upon policies adopted by governments toward oil production and conservation. Mr. Ralph W. Gallagher discussed some of these broad problems in the 1943 annual report to stockholders and concluded:

> The principal post-war problems of the Company and its affiliates, as we see them, will be (1) to re-employ and train the thousands of men and women who have gone into the armed forces, (2) to reconstruct distribution and marketing facilities, (3) to convert wartime refining and manufacturing facilities to peace-time production, (4) to help to expand the world's known oil reserves in step with an expanding worldwide need, (5) to reconstruct our world transportation systems. These problems are under constant study. Company affiliates expect to be able to convert to peace-time production quickly when permitted to do so.

Top Management Organization — Directors and Executives

The men responsible in 1944 for guiding Jersey through the problems suggested above were the board of directors of the parent company. All the board members were full-time employees whose duties were as directors, not operating officers. This situation was the outgrowth of a long evolution of management methods.

The functions of the parent company were defined as follows in an office memorandum issued July 1, 1944.

> The JERSEY Parent Company is a holding company, merely owning securities of other corporations, except for direct ownership of tankers and shipping facilities useful to its subsidiaries.

The Parent Company's principal business is constantly to study and review investments previously made or proposed by its Management, on behalf of the JERSEY stockholders, and to assure that all subsidiaries have capable managements and receive such aid or advice as they may need from time to time.

In such matters as consolidated accounting and finance, legal and tax advice, employee benefit plans, and governmental and public relations, JERSEY provides the centralized supervision which is essential for protection of its affiliated interests. It also encourages coordination in the operations of its subsidiaries for their mutual benefit, and provides advisory coordinators for that purpose. But so far as feasible, the directors and officers of each subsidiary are expected to manage its business autonomously. In this way JERSEY seeks continually to develop among its affiliates a large body of experienced executives, which is one of its principal assets.

As of July 1, 1944, the directors, the number of shares owned, and the year they were first elected directors were as shown in Exhibit 7. The directors owned 0.08% of the total number of shares outstanding.

All directors before being elected had had experience within the company and its subsidiaries as technical experts or executives carrying heavy responsibility. One had been president of a large natural gas utility company; others had been presidents of large integrated oil companies; one had been deputy governor of a large bank; another had been chief fiscal officer of an international company; another had been professor in a technical professional school and a director of industrial research; and another director had been an expert in employee relations. The directors had served Jersey an average of 28½ years.

During the five years prior to July 1, 1944, six new directors had been elected: two when board membership was increased from nine to eleven, and the other four to fill vacancies caused by death or retirement. Directors came under the pension and retirement plan covering all employees. This plan called for retirement at the age of 65.

The board had developed some fairly definite criteria and procedures in selecting nominees for directors. The Certificate

EXHIBIT 7. STANDARD OIL COMPANY (NEW JERSEY): INFORMATION REGARDING DIRECTORS

Name	Principal Occupation	First Elected Director	Shares Owned* April 15, 1944
F. W. Abrams	Vice President; Director	1940	1,250
F. H. Bedford, Jr.	Director	1927	7,448†
J. E. Crane	Director	1944	500
R. W. Gallagher	Chairman	1933	3,000
O. Harden	Vice President; Director	1929	2,023
R. T. Haslam	Director	1942	1,849
E. Holman	President; Director	1940	2,818
T. C. McCobb	Director	1935	800
F. W. Pierce	Director	1942	348
W. E. Pratt	Vice President; Director	1937	753
C. F. Smith	Director	1944	290

*The directors owned no securities of the company other than capital stock.

†This includes 2,829 shares held in trusts in which Mr. Bedford had only a life interest in the income and also 3,546 shares held in other trusts of which he was a trustee and in which he had contingent future beneficial interests.

SOURCE: Proxy Statement, 1944, and Company Sources.

of Incorporation gave the board power to fill vacancies until the next annual meeting of stockholders. Annually, the board listed nominees in its solicitation of proxies from stockholders, and stockholders voted for them at the annual meeting. The directors kept constantly on the alert for qualified men so they would be prepared, when occasion required, to suggest to stockholders a man well fitted to the company's needs. The board considered a man's experience, judgment, and ability to comprehend the ramifications of the complex, world-wide business, including the political climate in foreign countries. It also emphasized his ability to share ultimate responsibility for the whole organization, and endeavored to find men whose background would supplement that of the other directors. The board also considered the age of members on the board and of possible nominees so that as directors retired, the board would pass down from generation to generation an accumulating skill, knowledge, and technique of management. Finally, a director must be congenial to the rest of the board to ensure successful group action.

Recognizing that the company's junior executives as a group had a pretty sound understanding of the company and the problems of the oil industry, directors continually kept such

EXHIBIT 8. STANDARD OIL COMPANY (N. J.)
Condensed Organization Chart as of July 1, 1944

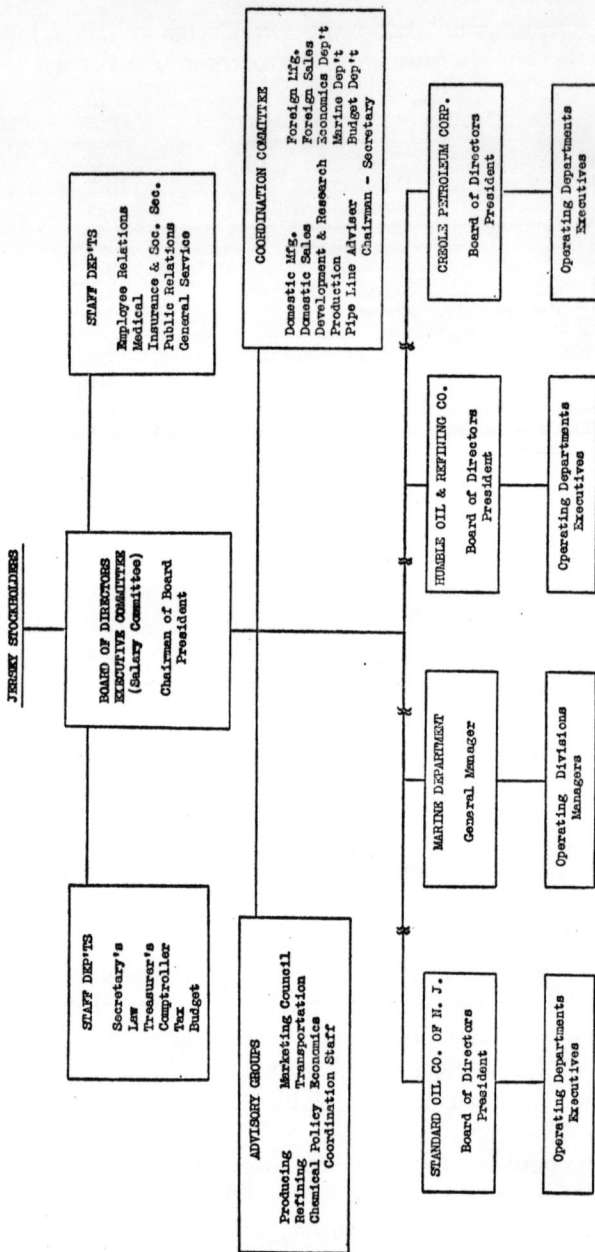

JERSEY STOCKHOLDERS

BOARD OF DIRECTORS
EXECUTIVE COMMITTEE
(Salary Committee)

Chairman of Board
President

STAFF DEP'TS

Employee Relations
Medical
Insurance & Soc. Sec.
Public Relations
General Service

STAFF DEP'TS

Secretary's
Law
Treasurer's
Comptroller
Tax
Budget

ADVISORY GROUPS

Producing   Marketing Council
Refining   Transportation
Chemical Policy Economics
Coordination Staff

COORDINATION COMMITTEE

Domestic Mfg.   Foreign Mfg.
Domestic Sales   Foreign Sales
Development & Research Economics Dep't
Production   Marine Dep't
Pipe Line Adviser Budget Dep't
Chairman – Secretary

STANDARD OIL CO. OF N. J.

Board of Directors
President

Operating Departments
Executives

MARINE DEPARTMENT

General Manager

Operating Divisions
Managers

HUMBLE OIL & REFINING CO.

Board of Directors
President

Operating Departments
Executives

CREOLE PETROLEUM CORP.

Board of Directors
President

Operating Departments
Executives

executives moving up into positions of greater responsibility and eventually put some of them on the board. Through the process of reviewing operations, it always had in mind a group of 100 or more executives eligible for constantly increasing responsibility.

The board had redefined its functions from time to time in the evolution of Jersey into a holding company. One director called the director's job a professional one requiring professional training. He pointed out that men who had previously been operating executives must acquire a new point of view on becoming directors. He said that Jersey made a distinction, also, between functions of directors and those of expert consultants. For special problems, such as foreign exchange, marketing, or public relations, the board hired executives or professional consultants. The board held that its functions were to develop men in the operating companies by giving them authority and responsibility; to keep themselves informed of subsidiaries' operations, particularly if they were isolated; to learn of troubles before they got big; to provide means for coordination and development of subsidiaries; to determine major policies; and to carry explanation of established policies to subsidiary executives.

The board adopted a policy against directors' or executives' serving on the board of other companies.

In the office memorandum dated July 1, 1944, previously referred to, there was set forth the organization of directors and officers. Exhibit 8 is an abstract of the chart accompanying the memorandum. An unusual plan was the assignment of specific "contacts" to each director. The following are excerpts:

BOARD OF DIRECTORS OF THE PARENT COMPANY. In discharging their responsibility to the stockholders, the JERSEY directors:

(1) Review director and officer personnel of each affiliate before granting a proxy for the annual election of directors in that affiliate. As a part of this review, changes may be suggested to strengthen management and provide new training opportunities....

(2) Consider and advise on subsidiary appropriations for major capital expenditures.

(3) Review financial results of subsidiaries' and affiliates' operations. At least once during each year, the management of each major operating subsidiary is invited to discuss operating results, financial reports (assisted by an analysis by the Comptroller), and future prospects. . . .

(4) Visit and inspect the properties of subsidiaries periodically.

The Board members are all available for consultation by the operating managements and advisory staffs. All members endeavor to be familiar with the business as a whole; but for greater convenience and efficiency in consultation, one particular Board member and an alternate are designated. . .for consultation with respect to each group of subsidiaries and major investments and each division of the Company's own organization. Directors should be consulted on operating or administrative problems only when they are deemed important. Consultation with the Board on policies affecting relations with stockholders, employees, customers, the general public and governments would appear advantageous in maintaining a broadly uniform and consistent result. . . .

The Board members consult, or receive as guests, prominent public leaders and independent experts in various fields, in order to keep informed of changing trends and viewpoints. . . .

EXECUTIVE COMMITTEE OF THE PARENT COMPANY. This Committee of Directors [the chairman, president, and two vice presidents] functions almost daily for the Board, between its meetings, reporting its actions at weekly meetings of the Board. All directors of the Parent Company are invited to attend Executive Committee meetings at any time. [Through the Charter and By-Laws the committee had the powers of the board of directors.]

EXECUTIVE OFFICERS OF THE PARENT COMPANY. All executive action taken by the Company flows through the Officers, who also consider and determine all questions not requiring the attention of the Board or Executive Committee in administration of the Parent Company's business. . . .

SUBSIDIARY COMPANY MANAGEMENTS. . . .Subsidiaries having outstanding minority interests are. . .required to operate autonomously in whatever manner their directors deem to the advantage of all of their stockholders.

Subsidiary managements will desire freely to consult the Parent Company's Board or advisory staff, not only to obtain

[96]

the benefit of their experience and skill but also as a means of coordination with the advice and procedures followed by other affiliated companies. By this means, and particularly through the Coordination Committee mentioned below, can be achieved a free interchange of ideas and experience that will be mutually beneficial to all subsidiaries.

COORDINATION COMMITTEE. This Committee is appointed by the JERSEY Executive Committee [only the chairman of the committee is a director].... It includes representatives of some subsidiaries as well as the Parent Company, and is designed as a study and advisory group to assist operating managements in planning and in meeting business problems. It is not an executive body nor authorized to make executive decisions for any company. Each member designates an alternate who will substitute when he is absent.

In addition to advising subsidiary management, the Coordination Committee will advise the Executive Committee of JERSEY on matters which it has studied and which require Parent Company consideration.

The Coordination Committee will meet regularly at times fixed by it, welcome JERSEY Board members and representatives of subsidiary companies at its meetings and from time to time may call upon members of JERSEY's departments or advisory staffs to assist in its deliberations.

...subcommittees [domestic, foreign, and chemical affairs] will deal with day to day operating questions and with over-all short range programs. Their personnel will be selected from time to time by the Chairman of each such subcommittee.

The Coordination Committee as a whole will deal directly with *long-range problems* on a world-wide basis, and will project tentative world-wide programs from time to time, in order that it may most effectively fulfill its function of advising JERSEY and JERSEY subsidiaries for their mutual benefit....

MARKETING COUNCIL. This group, appointed by the JERSEY Executive Committee, provides a forum where marketing executives of affiliated companies (for other than chemical or specialty products) may discuss marketing policies and make recommendations to the Coordination Committee or to the operating companies concerned. The Council may also make recommendations to the JERSEY Executive Committee on matters which require Parent Company consideration.

The Marketing Council in addition performs functions as

to marketing similar to those performed as to producing by the Coordinator of Producing Activities, and as to refining by the Coordinators of Refining Activities.

JERSEY ADVISORS. The Parent Company maintains a suitable advisory staff of experts in the various functions of the oil business, which will also be available to operating managements, for advice in their particular lines. This advisory staff is part of the JERSEY company and is responsible to the JERSEY Board, reporting through such department heads or coordinators of producing, manufacturing or sales activities as may be appointed. The principal groups... [are shown in Exhibit 8.]

This entire memorandum has been designed to explain the attached organization chart [Exhibit 8 is an abstract of the full chart] to those named in it, in order to facilitate its use by them and by their office associates who may need to refer to it. It should be borne in mind that the chart is dated July 1, 1944, and will be subject to change from time to time, due to the constant changes in organization both within the Parent Company and in subsidiary companies. This chart has been prepared for office use only, and in its preparation it has been necessary to omit many details and to over-simplify the organization structure.

Chairman of the Board of Directors and President

The office of chairman of the board was on a basis independent of, and unrelated to, succession from the presidency, as described in the following brief summary.

Mr. Alfred C. Bedford, president of the company at the time of World War I, was appointed chairman of the Petroleum Committee of the Council of National Defense. So that he could devote more time to this work of national importance, he was elected chairman of Jersey, and Mr. Walter C. Teagle was made president. Upon the death of Mr. Bedford, Mr. George H. Jones, who had been treasurer, was made chairman and continued in this office until his death in November, 1928. Mr. Teagle continued as president without a chairman of the board until 1933, when Mr. William S. Farish, who had been a director and president of an affiliate, was elected chairman. In 1937, Mr. Farish was elected president, and when Mr. Teagle retired, he was elected chairman, in which capacity he served until 1942. At that time Mr. Ralph W. Gallagher, who had been a vice president, was elected chairman of the board. When Mr. Farish suddenly died later in 1942, however, Mr. Gallagher was elected president and the office of chairman was left vacant. In 1944, Mr. Eugene Holman was elected president, and Mr. Gallagher once more became chairman of the board.

The by-laws defined the duties of the chairman and president as follows:

> The chairman of the board shall preside at all meetings of stockholders and directors. He shall have general care and supervision of the affairs of the company and in the absence of the president shall exercise the powers and duties of the president.
>
> The president, subject to the board of directors, shall be the chief executive officer of the company. In the absence of the chairman, he shall preside at meetings of the stockholders and directors and exercise the powers and duties of the chairman.

Methods of Communication

The office memorandum previously mentioned included a discussion of the contact assignments of directors. This plan of contact was unique. These assignments should be distinguished from the usual assignments of functional responsibilities to staff executives. The director assigned as contact for the board with a particular function had no authority over the department carrying out that function. The department remained responsible to the board. The contact assignment was the device through which the board, as a whole, sought close understanding with staff organizations and operating managements. Such assignments covered not only staff functions but also all the other major functions of the system.

The contact assignments did not take the place of responsibility and action by the board as a whole. The announcement of specific contacts, however, made sure that all the world-wide activities were covered. The board members recognized the sound understanding that operating executives had of problems in their respective fields and sought to keep informed of and take advantage of this understanding. They also sought to encourage the operating executives by assuring them of interest.

[99]

These contacts not only kept the board informed of management in the field but served to inform the operating management of major policies.

To emphasize further the difference between the director contacts and the functions of operating executives, one of the directors explained that the assignments did not limit the interest of other directors. The assignments were a channel of contact in contrast to customary channels of authority. Directors did not hesitate to discuss problems directly with staff departments or with subsidiary managements, even though these units were the assignment of another director.

Board and Executive Committee Meetings and Minutes

The Certificate of Incorporation and By-Laws authorized the board to appoint an Executive Committee with the powers of the board of directors between board meetings in the management of the business and the affairs of the company.

The board appointed four regular members and the rest of the board as alternates to take turns in serving as the fifth member. Three was a quorum. Other directors had a standing invitation to attend meetings and were asked particularly at times when the Executive Committee was discussing a question in a field in which one or more of them were specifically interested. Each director was responsible for bringing issues to the attention of the board. The four regular members currently were the chairman, president, and two vice presidents. The four regular members also constituted the Salary Committee, elsewhere discussed, and as such reported to the board through the Executive Committee's minutes.

The Executive Committee scheduled a meeting time each day, but usually convened on call from the secretary about three times a week as pending business dictated. The meetings ordinarily took about two hours. The secretary kept memoranda of discussions and minutes of decisions and consultations.

The full board met regularly once a week. However, the chairman or secretary called all board members to the Executive Committee meetings whenever an important issue was to come up which could not be held over to the regular board meeting day and when a special meeting of the board was not required. The full board deliberated on such questions as granting of proxies, review of subsidiary managements, capital budgets, and major questions of policy. At the weekly board meeting, each director had a copy of the memoranda and minutes of the Executive Committee. The secretary read the minutes of the Executive Committee. The board ordinarily accepted them, but occasionally initiated further deliberation. It also considered any resolutions legally required. Regular board meetings usually were shorter and more formal than those of the Executive Committee.

Problems Considered by the Board of Directors

The following summary of Executive Committee minutes for a week, picked at random, indicates the scope and variety of the problems considered by the committee and eventually by the board as a whole:

Received daily report of cash.

Approved filing returns with New York State Tax Department for ten subsidiaries.

Reviewed plan of subsidiary manufacturing department to install a secondhand bubble tower at estimated cost of $xx,ooo, which was in addition to the capital budget.

Executive reported discussion with State Department of the terms of proposed agreement between company and foreign company.

Executive reported that subsidiary had been granted foreign oil concession, for which negotiations had been under way for some time.

President reported he had been requested to appear before a hearing of Senate Military Affairs Subcommittee investigating monopoly restrictions on new scientific developments.

Executive summarized position in foreign country about oil concessions.

Reviewed profits for eight months.

Executive reported receipt of advice from subsidiary on result of Supreme Court litigation.

Subsidiary officers outlined details of proposed purchase by subsidiary of the —————— Oil Corporation for $xx,xoo,ooo. After discussion committee agreed proposed acquisition would be advantageous to subsidiary. Subsidiary men were present during the discussion.

Reviewed plan of subsidiary to install a new stair tower at estimated cost of $xx,ooo, an addition to its adopted 1943 Capital Budget.

Approved contributing —— to the —— —— Foundation. Salary Committee made report in detail of increases affecting —— companies.

Approved by cable granting proxies authorizing —— to vote company shares for following matters only:

(1) Approval of balance sheet.

(2) Declaring dividends.

(3) Authorization of payment of taxes on dividends.

Another director joined meeting and reported that —— City had authorized receipt of bids with respect to supply of motor fuel at Municipal Airport. Subsidiary contemplated joining with other oil companies in area in submitting a joint bid which would obligate each bidder to pay a flat sum in cash for concession in addition to —— per gallon of gas sold.

President reported subsidiary had decided to go ahead with project for expanding production at capital expenditure estimated at $xx,ooo,ooo.

Committee approved company subscribing for —— shares of preferred stock of —— Company.

President of subsidiary advised that Board of Directors and Officers intended to recommend special meeting of stockholders to amend charter to provide for —— shares of no par value instead of —— . Committee agreed and approved —— voting of shares at this meeting.

Secretary reported on Capital Budget for month and for nine months. Net additions were $xx,ooo,ooo making a total of $xxx,ooo,ooo compared with budget estimate of $xx,ooo,ooo.

Committee reviewed plan of subsidiary, Manufacturing Department, to convert furnace into steam boiler at Refinery. Estimated cost $xx,ooo, addition to Capital Budget, of which $xx,ooo would be charged to addition to budget and $x,ooo charged as expenses.

Problems Considered by Directors and Methods Used

The following illustrations were selected to indicate the methods used by the board.

On March 25, 1943, the board adopted the following resolutions:

RESOLVED, That the Regular Members of the Executive Committee shall constitute a Salary Committee whose duty it shall be to study and periodically to review salary levels for all executive employees of the Company and the policies governing the compensation of salaried employees of subsidiary and affiliated companies. The Salary Committee shall make periodic reports of its deliberations and the actions taken by it to the Board of Directors. The Salary Committee shall have the authority, within the limits hereinafter defined, to fix the salaries of all executive employees of the Company, including Members of the Board of Directors other than the Regular Members of the Executive Committee, the President and the Chairman of the Board; and

FURTHER RESOLVED, That, within the limits hereinafter defined, the salaries of the President and the Chairman of the Board shall be determined by the action of the Board of Directors; and

FURTHER RESOLVED, That, within the limits hereinafter defined, the President shall fix the salaries of the Regular Members of the Executive Committee; and

* * * * *

FURTHER RESOLVED, That, during the period in which this country is engaged in the present war no Director or Officer shall receive a salary in excess of $100,000 annually....

One means for freeing the board from the detail of operating problems was referring them to the Coordination Committee for advice. As described in the previous section on organization, this committee was composed of technical specialists, subsidiary executives, one director who acted as chairman, and a secretary. The board also encouraged operating managements to assume initiative. The contact assignments of directors as discussed under Methods of Communication also were designed to keep the board informed of problems without involving board members in administrative responsibilities. The board made an annual review of operating results for each subsidiary.

Also, the board annually selected the independent public accountants, subject to annual ratification by the stockholders.

The public accountants addressed their report to the stockholders and had a representative attend the annual meeting of stockholders.

The board recognized that the minority stockholders in certain subsidiaries might not always have quite their same point of view on questions. Therefore, it was careful to encourage the boards in subsidiaries to exercise independent judgment for the welfare of all their stockholders. The Jersey board had voted for outside directors in some subsidiaries when minority stockholders suggested competent nominees. This policy had been found of value, particularly in certain foreign subsidiaries, where the outside directors contributed to a mutual understanding between the community and the company.

The Jersey board also had felt a primary responsibility for developing a pension plan. The board believed that long-range developments, such as a pension plan, should be similar on a system-wide basis. The board wished to be able to encourage the transfer of executives among subsidiaries without penalizing the transferees. The board also took responsibility for ensuring the financial adequacy of the plan. When one of the directors called attention to current shortcomings of the existing plan, the board called for appointment of a committee to work out a revision. The chairman appointed the head of the Insurance and Social Security Department as chairman and made him responsible for producing an acceptable plan. To save time in the practical application of the plan, the board included on the committee, from the outset, the heads of the Tax, Legal, and Employee Relations Departments. The secretary was included for his experience as one of the administrators of the existing plan. The director who had the usual contact with the Employee Relations Department was named to provide general guidance.

The head of the Employee Relations Department informed affected subsidiaries of the project and got their opinions on proposals through their employee relations departments. In this way the operating companies affected became familiar with the growth of the plan and had an opportunity to present any additional features they felt necessary. The subsidiaries explored the provisions of the plan for their particular needs. The committee worked out technical aspects, then the Jersey board formally adopted the plan for the parent company. It recommended adoption for subsidiaries as being in the best interests of all concerned. The subsidiaries' boards of directors then passed formal resolutions adopting it and authorizing their officers to put it into effect.

All questions of foreign policy met by subsidiaries in the foreign field were usually discussed by subsidiary executives with the Jersey board. Relations entered into with I. G. Farbenindustrie were first reported to the stockholders in annual reports for the years ended December 31, 1928 and 1929, in paragraphs headed "A New Development" and "Hydrogenation." These statements explained that agreements had been made to gain the benefits of I. G. Farbenindustrie's fundamental research on the synthesis of organic compounds. Although no accurate estimate could be made for the future, the reports indicated discovery of new processes of substantial use in the oil industry and a more definite overlapping of the fields of the oil and chemical industries. The 1929 report outlined a plan for forming a new subsidiary patent-holding company. From time to time progress in the new processes was mentioned in annual reports.

Fourteen years after the first announcement, when the United States was at war with Germany, Mr. Thurman Arnold, who was in charge of antimonopoly investigations for the Department of Justice, made public charges against the company, its officers and directors, resulting, according to Mr. Farish, in "widespread misunderstanding of the company's operations, its international relations and their effect upon the war effort of the United States." Mr. Farish was called to testify before the Senate Committee to Investigate the National Defense Program. He sent an explanatory letter to stockholders and employees on April 9, 1942, enclosing a copy of his testimony answering each of these charges. He explained that the agreements made in 1929 with I. G. Farbenindustrie had been the subject of an antitrust proceeding in 1941. The company had accepted a consent decree, in view of wartime conditions, and terminated the contracts in question. The court affirmed the personal loyalty of the directors and officers to the United States. Mr. Farish explained to a questioning stockholder at the annual meeting which followed, on June 2, 1942, that the Department of Justice had examined 110,000 different company documents, letters, memoranda, and contracts, and had selected a little over 40,000 for its purposes. He pointed out that in such a complex question there was lack of fairness in basing conclusions on only part of the data.

On another matter involving policy in the foreign field and bearing on the company's relations with France, Italy, Iraq, and Latin American countries, Mr. Gallagher, then president, made a statement on May 23, 1944, before the O'Mahoney Subcommittee of the Senate Committee on the Judiciary. The problem facing Standard Oil Company (New Jersey) was summarized by Mr. Gallagher in this statement as follows:

> We are therefore in this position: The United States practices a system of free and open competition in business. Most other countries operate, to greater or lesser degree, under controlled economies. As a result, when Americans have done business in those countries they have had to work under such systems of control. For doing this, many of them have been severely and widely criticized.
>
> What can be done to resolve this disparity between our own and foreign laws, between wanting Americans to do business abroad but holding constantly over them the stigma of acting against the American public interest?

The Jersey board assumed responsibility for observing whether investments in the different subsidiaries yielded an adequate return and that due provision was made for ultimate return of the capital investment.

The manner in which the directors fulfilled this function was illustrated by one executive in a description of a typical expansion in refinery capacity of a subsidiary and the manner in which it was reviewed along with all other items of budgeted capital expenditures. This project was initiated, as were most similar operating projects, by the management staff of the subsidiary.

The refinery manager of the subsidiary reported to his president that more crude was available than it had capacity to handle. He also noted that product quality could be improved with new equipment and that the existing refinery was becoming obsolete in certain respects. To meet this situation, he recommended a program for spending $x,000,000 for increasing capacity and modernizing refinery facilities, to take about six months to complete.

The president of the subsidiary made preliminary investigations, which indicated that the program had promise, and got tentative assurance from the subsidiaries to whom it would normally sell the output that the increased supply would be taken. The staff of the subsidiary then worked up the program in more detail, and the president included it in the budget he submitted to his own board of directors.

In August of each year the budget department of the parent company sent out to each subsidiary a budget manual for the following calendar year with forms to be returned by October 1. The marketing and manufacturing capital expenditure budgets described projects in considerable detail, including items down to $200. Budgets for producing and pipeline expenditures were part of a continuing world-wide program and were approved as part of this plan. Producing and pipeline budgets were on a "program" rather than an "item" basis.

The subsidiary board approved the inclusion of the project and sent its program of "contemplated action" to the Coordination Committee of the Jersey company. This committee looked at the items in this contemplated budget in relation to the programs of the other subsidiaries which might have to increase facilities for transportation or marketing before the system could realize the advantages of this increased refinery capacity and other proposals. In the light of this study, the Coordination Committee suggested minor adjustments for consideration of the subsidiary.

When the Coordination Committee was doubtful about the current advisability of a program, it referred it to the Executive Committee. On projects of some magnitude the procedure was to have representatives of the subsidiary and the Coordination Committee sit in with the Executive Committee and other directors for a final hearing. Should the project then seem unwise, the secretary would write a letter to the president of the subsidiary to the effect that, in the opinion of the board, prudent management would not go through with the project in view of the current outlook.

After any further comments from subsidiaries, the Coordination Committee submitted the adjusted contemplated subsidiaries' budgets to the Jersey board. In such important meetings all board members were usually present for discussion. They considered the probable return, funds available in the subsidiary or in the system as a whole, the wisdom of outside borrowing, and the general over-all attractiveness of the project. Finding these satisfactory, the committee in this case agreed to the desirability of the budgets as submitted, and transmitted its views to the subsidiaries. In almost all instances the next step was that the subsidiaries' boards of directors then formally adopted their respective budgets to guide their executives.

The Jersey directors had established a ruling for all subsidiaries that for all projects costing more than $100,000, a final re-examination by the Jersey board should be made before the money was actually spent, even though the project had already been included in the adopted budget. This provision was to make sure, in view of the inevitable lapse of time, that the over-all desirability of the project had not changed. (This review before actual expenditure did not apply to producing and pipeline programs.)

Therefore, in the case of the refinery project being used for illustration, when it came time to spend the money, the president of the subsidiary referred the proposal to the Coordination Committee again to see if any of the technical groups or other operating groups in the system had found conditions which would change the advisability of the expenditure. This reference was made on a standard form of appropriation. The Coordination Committee was still satisfied, but it nevertheless referred its comments to the Executive Committee to see if that committee had any further observations. This total procedure of review before expenditure took about a month.

In contrast to the preceding illustration, in which the initiative came from an operating subsidiary, the Jersey directors of the holding company took the initiative in starting postwar plans for the entire system. In a sense this was a modification of a prewar plan of periodic five-year projections. The board called for contemplated capital requirements from each subsidiary for the two years following the end of the war. This request had been preceded by informal discussions within the board and with various members of the parent and subsidiary organizations. The Coordination Committee acted as administrative aide for the board on this project. In conjunction with the budget department, it referred the request to all advisory groups and subsidiaries.[1]

In this case the Coordination Committee classified the contemplated capital expenditures of subsidiaries by functions rather than by corporate bodies, the primary functions being production, refining, transportation, marketing, and research. The Coordination Committee finally submitted a composite picture to the board. The chief purposes of this work, in the opinion of some directors, were: (1) to stimulate the imaginative planning of all subsidiaries for the future; (2) to make sure that, finally, the same point of view toward expenditures could be taken; (3) to allow the Jersey board to plan financing of the program. The board considered dividend policies. It also studied sources of new capital, either through the subsidiaries or the parent company or banks. When the Jersey board was satisfied that it had reconciled all these points of view, it made available to all affected subsidiaries and departments the revised contemplated budget expenditures.

The board did not limit its interests to financial plans, however. It considered that the company's greatest asset and strength was a loyal, experienced, and able personnel. It fixed responsibility for operations on subsidiaries' executives, and reviewed their accomplishments at least annually.

The management of each subsidiary was required to submit to the Jersey board nominees for the subsidiary's directors and officers one month before the annual meeting of the subsidiary. The managements supported their proposals by organization charts giving for each executive a brief statement of his responsibilities, functions, age, nationality, and salary. The Executive Committee and the director assigned as contact for

[1]See previous explanation of organization, pp. 96 and 97.

the subsidiary studied and usually discussed the proposals with the subsidiary's management. In this way, the board made the granting of proxies to subsidiaries a formal occasion for checking the over-all development of executive personnel and any other organization problems affecting the subsidiary.

The preceding illustrations were selected not as a sample cross section of all issues coming before the Jersey board, but to emphasize certain leading characteristics of the board in action. Of necessity they were oversimplified and taken from their context of time and personalities, without which there could be but partial comprehension of the directors and their functions.

Reports of Management to Stockholders

The management sent stockholders not only the usual financial statements, but also explanations of various matters affecting profits and company operations in general. In addition it sent out informative proxy statements, copies of statements executives had made before Congressional committees, material prepared to explain company policy to employees, and copies of *The Lamp*, an illustrated company magazine carrying petroleum news for employees and stockholders.

The evolution of annual reports to stockholders, from the first sparse balance sheet sent out in 1919 covering the year 1918 to the comprehensive analysis currently given, was in itself a part of the company's history of the last 25 years. The annual report sent to stockholders dated April 25, 1944, carried statistics about operations; an analysis of earnings, dividends, and assets; and paragraphs under the following headings: FINANCIAL: Volume, Consolidated Earnings, Parent Company Earnings, Dividends and Distribution of Assets, Renegotiation, Investment in Plant and Equipment, Capital Expenditures for War, Funded and Long-Term Debt, Working Capital, Payroll, Mexican Settlement, Segregation of Natural Gas Companies; WAR: 100-Octane Gasoline, Synthetic Toluene, Synthetic Rubber; PRODUCTION: Crude Oil Reserves, A World Oil Policy, Creole Petroleum Corporation, Arctic Oil; MANUFACTURING; MARKETING; TRANSPORTATION: Pipelines, Marine; RESEARCH: Buna Rubber Licensing Agreement, Butyl Rubber;

INDUSTRIAL RELATIONS: Employee Security, Employee Relations; POSTWAR: AN APPRECIATION. These topics were illustrated by charts and pictures of employees at work.

Starting in 1942, a two-year comparative financial statement was included with the annual report at the suggestion of a stockholder at the preceding annual meeting. The annual meetings had become increasingly a forum at which stockholders discussed the company's affairs with management. The attendance in 1944 was over 300.

CHAPTER VIII

Comparisons

THE four case studies, which were made in 1944-1945, make possible a comparison of directors functioning in companies with different backgrounds. Although all four companies were profitable, a comparison shows great variation in the subjects covered in the cases. Analysis also reveals that the way each of these factors was treated by each company depended largely on the differences in the backgrounds of the companies. Similarities in functioning were limited mainly to fulfilling legal requirements. These differences suggest that if no formal pattern for directors is forced on corporations by legislation, there is little likelihood of close conformity or little need for it.

Personalities Were Dominant Factors

In any comparison of the directorates and executive groups of various companies, their organization and functioning, the one factor which transcends all others is the human element — the personality, ability, and energy of the individuals involved. Irrespective of rules, regulations, or organization, the personalities and thinking of these men place their imprint on all corporate practices and policies. The history of The American Tobacco Company, for instance, pointed to the influence of a colorful, forceful president. The history of Climax Molybdenum Company could be described as that of the pioneering personalities involved. The character of General Foods Corporation was set by a group of forceful and able executive-directors backed by a large stockholder and prominent outside directors. Standard Oil Company (New Jersey) was dominated by a group of directors who had developed a philosophy of trusteeship and who had had experience in getting things done.

Board Organization and Policies Differed with Business Problems

One of the basic differences shown in the cases is in the industrial environment of the companies. American Tobacco bought tobacco leaf and manufactured and sold tobacco products through wholesale-retail channels of distribution to consumers. Under a policy of concentration based on experience and adopted with deliberation, its main efforts were devoted to the promotion of the single brand, Lucky Strike. In contrast, Climax concentrated on the commercial development of molybdenum through metallurgical research. It sold its products primarily to iron and steel producers, who ordered on specification of their industrial customers. General Foods, which produced a wide range of grocery specialty products, was concerned with the problems of mass selling, generally through common channels of distribution to consumers. The Jersey organization dealt with the single raw material, petroleum, and had world-wide ramifications in the production, transportation, refining, and marketing of this commodity and innumerable by-products and related products.

The organization of the directorates in the four companies was influenced by these differences in industrial background as well as by ownership, traditions, and management personalities. Climax, for instance, had few policies applying to directors because of its size and comparatively compact group of directors and stockholders. Directors and their associates still owned about half the capital stock. There were seven board members, two executives and five nonexecutives. The company had no permanent committees, not even the common executive committee. The board met monthly. At the other extreme was Jersey, which had numerous policies varying all the way from specific requirements that a director must be a full-time employee but removed from operations to a prohibition against any director's being a director of another company. The board met weekly and the executive committee, daily. In addition there were other committees of directors. Specific assignments were made to each director for maintaining contact with the world-wide operating units.

The practice of American Tobacco was not to elect outside men to its board, although in the 1920's there had been two outside members and a board chairman. There were 17 directors, each of whom was an executive. Its executives were not permitted to serve on other boards of directors. The board was not organized into committees. Meetings were scheduled weekly, but actually the board convened only when business required it. In contrast, a majority of the directors of General Foods were not executives of the company. Directors served on regular and special committees and consulted with executives from time to time. Directors held 107 other directorships, and executives were encouraged to serve on other boards for the broadening experience.

Only two of the companies had board chairmen, and duties of these two officers varied. The chairman of General Foods Corporation was also the chief executive, but not the president. As chairman, he represented the stockholders' point of view, brought to the board questions of policy, followed up board decisions, informed the board of executive action and changes in personnel, took the lead in filling vacancies, officiated at meetings, and appointed committees. The office of chairman of Jersey was considered by tradition to be independent of succession from the presidency. The by-laws provided that the chairman should preside at meetings and be responsible for the general care and supervision of the company.

Methods of Communication Varied with Organization

Methods had been developed in each company to keep the board informed of problems arising out of new or changing conditions, and to communicate directors' decisions to the operating organization, but there was little similarity in their practices. American Tobacco directors carried policy decisions into the operating organization in their capacity as executives. They conferred with the president on problems and questions of policy. Although some of the directors of Climax were outside, all had a background knowledge of operations through their past experience with the company. The board was small, and many questions were cleared with directors by means of telephone calls and informal meetings. On major questions executives submitted memoranda to directors before board meetings.

In General Foods, directors and executives jointly developed a procedure whereby directors would be kept informed of operations so that they could effectively meet their responsibilities. The chairman prepared agenda for board meetings covering issues for discussion and decision, minutes of the executive committee for confirmation, reports of executive action, and financial statistics.

Since directors in Jersey spent their full time as directors, unique arrangements had been developed for board operation. Each director had his specific "contact" assignment. In addition, the board reviewed the capital budgets of subsidiaries, and the board also reviewed operating results and personnel when granting proxies to subsidiary managements. Reports from the Coordination Committee and advisory groups created by the board kept it informed on current developments affecting subsidiaries and long-range programs.

Top executive management in each company was organized to meet the individual administrative and operating problems raised by the differences in industrial environment. The president of American Tobacco, the chief executive, had broad responsibility for the operation of all departments and activities. Each director had specific responsibilities in operations in his capacity of executive; the top five were a vice president in charge of sales, a vice president in charge of advertising, a vice president who was president of an important subsidiary, a chief of manufacture, and the president of a subsidiary in charge of buying leaf tobacco. Administration of Climax was through the president, senior vice president, and three operating vice presidents, with a metallurgical committee to coordinate manufacture and research. In General Foods the chairman of the board was the chief executive. The president was responsible for coordination, and the executive vice president for operations. The three senior executives were assisted by nine service vice presidents, four operating vice presidents, and subsidiary company managements. Since operations in Jersey were the province of the subsidiaries and operating departments, the parent board of 11 directors attempted to give them operating autonomy. The chairman of the board was responsible for broad public relationships and for maintaining effective director contacts. The president was the chief executive officer.

Action by the Board and by Individual Directors

Various aspects of top management organization have been contrasted and shown in relation to each company's corporate background. Comparisons also can be drawn showing how directors handled trusteeship obligations which arose in performance of duties involving broad questions of relationships with the stockholders, creditors, employees, the public, and government agencies, particularly in issues or problems which might have involved a conflict of interest between directors personally and their duties to these groups.

Problems were selected to show each board's approach to its management responsibilities. These problems were not a complete cross-section for any of the companies. The Jersey board's philosophy was expressed in its recognition of its trusteeship duties. Directors of the company tried to remove themselves from all operations so that they could concentrate on the over-all policies of the company and check the progress of the operating executives. When conflicts might have arisen between the personal interests of a director and his duties to the company, directors devised methods to avoid self-dealing. They spent their full time at their duties, one of which was to visit subsidiaries. They approved financial budgets, consulted with executives, and checked constantly on operating results and the character of subsidiary management.

The General Foods board approached its trusteeship problems in a different manner. The majority of its board members were experienced executives of other companies. The chairman assumed responsibility for submitting to directors adequate data to familiarize them with the current problems faced by the company. Directors served on committees, visited plants, and were available for consultation. Committees of directors were responsible for problems involving conflicts of interest or possibilities of self-dealing.

The directors of American Tobacco voted on matters which came before them at formal meetings. As a group they were responsible for submitting to the stockholders, for the stockholders' approval each year, their candidates for the next year's board of directors, and, when such approval was given by stockholders' election, the new board elected the president and other officers. In Climax, the directors, who were substantial owners, determined executive compensation and policies for labor and public relations.

The extent to which directors were concerned with administration was another point of variation among the companies and reflected differences in organization. Directors of Jersey utilized the broad administrative experience and skill of various board members. Directors reviewed the results of operating companies. They took responsibility for seeing that personnel changes were made in recognition of exceptional merit or to correct unsatisfactory conditions. But they did not have operating responsibilities. The American Tobacco practices were almost the reverse of those in Jersey. Administrative functions were the province of the directors, for they were also executives. Indeed, all final decisions resided in the president and his staff of director-executives. Most of the Climax directors had had administrative experience in the company, and although they delegated action to executives, they frequently consulted with them on· questions of policy. General Foods had placed its administrative functions in the control of its executives; the chairman was the chief executive. The executives, in conjunction with the Executive Council, operated the company and frequently consulted board members on special issues.

Board Minutes and Meetings Inadequate Measure of Directors' Contribution

The minutes of board meetings recorded formal action required by law, as well as action on individual company problems. Board action was the result, ordinarily, of unanimous decision. This fact, however, did not mean that directors were complacent and always gave automatic approval to proposals. As one board secretary explained, before executives submitted proposals to the board, they made sure they had adequately covered the problem involved so that they could answer any questions directors might ask.

The subjects dealt with at board meetings in all four companies were by no means the full measure of participation by directors in management functions. Board minutes of American Tobacco, in addition to the formal action required by law, included action on salary increases. The Climax board's minutes included memoranda submitted by officers recommending projects, and operating and financial statistics, in addition to legally required matter. The General Foods minutes included reports on deliberation and decisions of the board, the minutes of the Executive Committee as approved, the report of operations by the chairman, and statistical information. Board minutes of Jersey covered formal action and the approval of budgets and proxies of subsidiaries.

The one record common to all four companies was the formal minutes of directors' meetings. Records supporting the minutes varied greatly. Executive committees also kept detailed records, which were read and approved at subsequent board meetings.

Reports of Management to Stockholders

American Tobacco's financial statements were sent to stockholders with a brief covering paragraph from the treasurer. These reports were supplemented by letters from the president to stockholders discussing important corporate developments. At times the information was presented in booklets or in copies of advertising material. Sometimes a carton of cigarettes was sent with a letter urging stockholders to help the growth of business by distributing them and recommending them to their friends. In Climax, the stock had only recently begun to have wide distribution, and the reports accompanying financial statements were brief. These were supplemented on special occasions by letters authorized by the board of directors. General Foods amplified the annual financial report with illustrations, descriptions of operations, and comments on problems. It also sent letters to stockholders about unusual events. In Jersey, the annual report was part of a booklet describing operating results and factors affecting the business. In addition, the company sent stockholders copies of *The Lamp*, published for them and employees, which described major developments in the company and the oil industry. It also furnished copies of statements made by executives on occasions such as investigations and litigation.

It is impossible and unnecessary to conclude from an analysis of the four companies that one company was better off or more fortunate than another because of the way its board was organized and functioned. To suggest, for example, that The American Tobacco Company would be more profitable if it followed Standard Oil Company (New Jersey), or that Standard Oil Company (New Jersey) would be more successful if it developed a pattern of management like General Foods Corporation, or that Climax Molybdenum Company needed the complex organization of other companies is to overlook tradition, human nature, and business requirements and to stray far from reality. The comparisons, however, do reveal that any one of a variety of directorate setups can contribute to profitable operations.

CHAPTER IX

The Board Chairman: A Challenge

How can a board of directors be made more effective? This question is a challenge to directors, stockholders, board chairmen, chief executives, and anyone else studying or working with this issue. This chapter outlines the problem of increasing board effectiveness through adequate leadership and the consequent challenge to the board chairman, whether he is the chief executive or a separate officer.

The concepts of the board chairman encountered in this whole research, not just the four companies cited, varied so widely as to be practically meaningless. The title suggested anything from a promoted but ineffective president to a strong chief executive. The confusion was not always just in the meaning of titles. It also existed in the division of top management duties between the chairman and the chief executive. When the board chairman and the chief executive were the same individual, the chairman's functions were sometimes neglected; or, if the chairman was not the chief executive, often no adequate working relationship or understanding of his duties had been developed. There appeared to be a trend toward more frequent use of the title and toward electing a separate chairman. Moreover, the trend seems likely to continue as companies grow larger, top management functions become increasingly complex, and pension plans lead to earlier retirement of chief executives. Defining the duties of the chairman is an important first step in improving the performance of directorates.

The full difficulty of even stating the problem became apparent in discussions with numerous board chairmen and chief executives. Comments were frank and critical, as indicated by excerpts from those made by one chief executive.

> . . . I suggest that you stress a little more the conclusion that there are no established functions of a Chairman. I think it is

significant that numerous companies like the XYZ Company have had a Chairman of the Board sometimes and then discontinued the office for a while and then re-established it. Sometimes in the same company the functions of the Chairman are changed from time to time. It is all a matter of the problems of the time and the personalities of the men involved.

... the analogy came back to me which I have often maintained between a corporation and a football team ... Certainly a coach with a light, fast team would use a different system from a coach with a big, heavy team.

There is in a way a certain anomaly in having a Chairman of the Board. It calls for a division of executive responsibility and it is often very difficult for an organization to be run by two men. On the other hand, the personalities of the men may be such that a division of responsibilities may be very effectively accomplished. A President is so engrossed in operations that he often may be very glad to have someone to help him on the broader aspects, such as public relations.

Another point of view was given by Mr. Myron C. Taylor, Chairman of United States Steel Corporation, in the following statement in 1938:

Judge Elbert H. Gary, at the time of his death in 1927, was the Chief Executive Officer of the Corporation, as well as Chairman of the Board and Chairman of the Finance Committee. It did not seem wise to the Board of Directors to continue the concentration of these several offices in one person, especially since at that time I cherished the hope of being able to complete the reorganization of the Corporation and retire within five years. Under the new arrangement, I became Chairman of the Finance Committee in December, 1927, and Mr. James A. Farrell continued as President and also became Chief Executive Officer. Mr. J. P. Morgan acted as Chairman of the Board but was not an executive officer. In 1932, for the first time, I became an executive officer, being elected Chairman of the Board and Chief Executive Officer, with Mr. William J. Filbert as Vice-Chairman and Mr. William A. Irwin as President. In 1933 Mr. Filbert succeeded me as Chairman of the Finance Committee....[1]

[1]Myron C. Taylor, *Ten Years of Steel*, Extension of Remarks, Annual Meeting of Stockholders of the United States Steel Corporation, Hoboken, New Jersey, April 4, 1938, p. 8.

When Mr. Taylor retired in 1938, Mr. Edward R. Stettinius, Jr., was made board chairman responsible for "general oversight"; Mr. Enders M. Voorhees, Finance Committee Chairman, responsible for "supervision of the financial affairs"; and Mr. Benjamin F. Fairless, president, was made "chief administrative officer."[1]

The B. F. Goodrich Company elected Mr. D. M. Goodrich chairman of the board of directors and Mr. H. Hough president in 1927 upon the death of Mr. Bertram G. Work, who had been chairman of the board and president. Mr. J. D. Tew was elected president in 1928, Mr. S. B. Robertson in 1937, and Mr. John L. Collyer in 1939. Mr. Goodrich continued as chairman.

Standard Brands Incorporated in its annual report for 1941 stated, "On December 19, 1941, James S. Adams was elected President, a Director and Chief Executive Officer of the Company. Thomas L. Smith became Chairman of the Board and will serve in an advisory capacity."

The chairman of another company before accepting election to the position insisted that his position be defined in the by-laws as follows:

> The Chairman of the Board of Directors, when present, shall preside at all meetings of the Board and shall act as consultant and as adviser of the officers. It shall be the duty of the officers to consult with the Chairman of the Board of Directors regarding all important matters of policy in the conduct of the business of the Corporation and in regard to all major financial transactions of the Corporation and if, upon such consultation, the Chairman of the Board of Directors shall disapprove a contemplated action, the action shall not be taken until the Board of Directors shall approve.

Another chairman felt that there would be real danger in formalizing his position as a permanent job, independent of succession from the chief executive. He saw difficulty in always being able to find a man to fill the position adequately without engendering friction with the chief executive. He stated that he could not write a plan for dividing the duties of the chair-

[1] *Fortune*, March, 1940, p. 65.

man from those of the chief executive until he knew who the men were.

Functions of the Board Chairman

In spite of the wide variations in practice, the preliminary evidence in the study pointed to certain functions of the board chairman that seem clear and distinct from those of the chief executive, whether or not one man fills both positions. The following paragraphs do not discuss the merits of having a separate officer called board chairman. The purpose of this section is to describe *functions that need to be performed by someone regardless of his title or other functions.*

The first duty of the board chairman is to convene and preside at board meetings. It is important to emphasize that directors have no legal power except as a convened board. The distinction between the authority of men as directors and as executives is important not only as a matter of law, but also in administrative practice. For instance, one experienced board chairman and chief executive stated: "When a director steps out of the board room he should have no authority. If he happens to be both a director and an officer of the company his authority within the organization is simply due to his executive office. . . . That is a distinction which needs to be watched sometimes. People down in an organization are apt not to know the distinction and to think a director as such has some authority over them. Sometimes the director himself does not realize the distinction, and I have seen cases where confusion within the organization resulted." The position of chairman as a presiding officer is not an executive one; it does not carry any individual executive authority, although through personal prestige the chairman may wield substantial influence.

Another function of the man acting as board chairman is to make the board effective in dealing with questions in which the trusteeship aspects are critical: for example, determining executive salaries, bonus plans, and pensions; selecting and electing directors; determining dividend policy; and selecting and dealing with auditors. Failure of the board to provide for discharging these functions in the past in some companies had led critics to say of directors: "No one is interested in stockholders."[1] "Officers employ auditors and check themselves." "Executive directors pay themselves large salaries and devise their own bonus and pension plans." "Directors are merely rubber stamps." The growing importance of these trusteeship aspects of business management on top of the already "killing tasks" of the chief executive is leading many large corporations to elect a chairman in addition to the chief executive. This new emphasis on trusteeship has begun to convert some chief executives who previously had been skeptical about the justification for a separate board chairman. This seems particularly true of chief executives who are approaching the retirement age. They foresee that the next generation of top management must not only discharge all the exacting duties of leading an organization, but must also find a way through the increasingly complex relations with stockholders and perplexing questions of labor and public policy. One concept of trusteeship functions[2] is shown in the "Functional Plan of Organization" prepared by the American Steel Foundries, of which Mr. Thomas Drever is president and board chairman. The two top management boxes on the company's organization chart contain the following explanations:

BOARD OF DIRECTORS

(Trusteeship management)
Representing, safeguarding and furthering stockholders' interests; determining basic policies and broad course of the business; reviewing and appraising over-all results.

ADMINISTRATIVE COMMITTEE

(General management)
Planning, directing, coordinating and controlling the business

[1]"On the agenda of a recent Chicago clinic on corporate public relations was a discussion of company directorates — how directors are selected, how they perform their functions, how much they are paid and what part they play in improving the company's vital contacts with stockholders and the public generally.... The letter of inquiry was sent in all cases [by *Chicago Journal of Commerce*] to the secretary of the company. Few of them troubled to send covering letters with their replies. Here, obviously, was an opportunity for a man with ideas on corporate public relations to elaborate on them. Only two took advantage of the opportunity." Wilbur J. Brons, "The Round Table," *Chicago Journal of Commerce*, October 9, 1943.

[2]See also charts in Holden, Fish, and Smith, *Top Management Organization and Control*, pp. 28 and 73.

as a whole; determining objectives; establishing company policies and securing results.

The president, serving as chairman, meets with vice presidents and president of Griffin [a subsidiary] each Monday morning for considering, coordinating and deciding matters of general concern.

A further function of the chairman is facilitating succession of management: perpetuation of management on the basis of merit rather than on mere seniority. In one large company where three vice presidents competed strenuously for the vacant presidency, an older fourth officer whom all respected was made chairman and maintained balance until the one selected for president proved his impartiality and ability to lead the entire organization. Many chief executives reported the great relief of having an older, experienced, responsible chairman with whom to discuss problems. The able chairman knows how to counsel without taking over administrative jobs. He recognizes that each executive has a distinct administrative personality and encourages a new chief executive to take over the active administration in his own way. The chairman leads the board in selecting the chief executive. The chairman cultivates executive growth and harmonious relations with the board by fostering the delegation of administrative authority and responsibility, by providing checks on executive performance, and by judicious selection of questions for board action.

Another of the chairman's important functions is keeping the board's attention directed to policy questions rather than administrative detail. This point of view was particularly difficult to maintain, according to one chief executive and board chairman. In his opinion, questions of general strategy occurred so infrequently in companies the size of his that board meetings tended to slip into the role of operating staff meetings. To his regret the intense requirements of competitive operations did not leave him time for the reflective thinking required for industrial statesmanship and for formulating long-range policies. Many chairmen expressed doubt that anyone who had not come up through the organization could recognize policy questions arising in a company. Difficult as it may be, it is part of the board chairman's job to sense the trend of minor decisions and bring the emerging policy to board attention for deliberate decision. He should prevent his company from drifting blindly by a succession of minor decisions into major policies.

The position of chairman as presiding officer calls for skill in drawing out directors' contributions to decisions. This skill is in distinct contrast to that required of the chief executive, namely, to explain, to persuade, to encourage, and to follow up individuals in the administration of policy. Without skill in opening questions for discussion, the chairman cannot be fully effective in bringing the judgment of directors to bear on issues presented to them. One chief executive reported that his board members were less free in their criticism of proposals when he was presiding at board meetings than when the chairman was presiding. When questions are skillfully presented, the sense of the board on the subject under consideration may suggest further investigation of alternatives. After such open discussion most boards generally come to unanimous agreement on major decisions.

One way to help avoid misunderstanding between directors and executives is for the chairman to work out standards of procedure with the board. These standards are to guide the executives when questions arise so that they will know under what circumstances the board wants to decide questions, or to give counsel, or to delegate authority for making decisions to executives subject to board confirmation or review. The basis for these standards must be sincere mutual regard by directors and executives for their respective obligations. Conflicts, confusion, and petty annoyances at this level must be avoided. The ordinary solution of drawing lines of responsibility and authority, however, is not valid because both directors and executives are part of top management and are responsible for the whole enterprise. The board chairman should make certain that all responsibilities of top management are being met, whether by the board or by executives. By working out definite procedures, a board can avoid complaints such as the following: "A chairman might compete for the loyalty of executive directors and interfere with the smooth functioning of the organization." "It is difficult to have two captains for one ship." "A separate chairman feels that he must get into operations to earn his salary." "A separate chairman might countermand or give conflicting orders." If procedures are clarified, many companies may require only a part-time chairman; his office may be located in a separate building or city for the convenience of the board. Furthermore, differences in compensation of the board chairman and the chief executive help stress the importance of the chief executive's drive, determination, vision, and position of leadership in the company.

A useful technique for the chairman is the development of agenda for board meetings. One chairman broke the agenda down into four parts: (1) issues on which the board should take initial jurisdiction and determine a solution; (2) issues on which the board must take formal action, but on which initiative had been exercised by executives and on which the board would merely check; (3) questions with which executives were confronted and on which they could profit by consultation with directors; (4) reports of executive action and other information that provided necessary background for directors.

The Man for Board Chairman

The purpose of this section is not to pose the question, Should the chief executive also be board chairman? Rather, the purpose here is again to direct attention to the conclusion drawn from the study of cases. Chapter III and also Chapter VIII pointed out the need for understanding any given case before one attempts to prescribe remedies. This is counseling not inactivity, but foresight, for the relation between cause and effect in corporate organization is complex. Further case studies are being made to clarify the bases for choice of board chairman and relations between the board chairman and the chief executive. The difficulty of understanding these relations, however, must not divert attention from the real need for top management to comprehend and discharge all its increasingly complex functions, those of trusteeship as well as those of administration.

If there is a chairman separate from the chief executive, constructive relations between the two men require clear understanding of the shifting line between their duties.

If one man is both chief executive and board chairman, he must definitely recognize his dual responsibility for carrying out his executive duties and for providing board leadership.

Finally, this analysis indicates the importance of the functions to be performed by the chairman of the board and suggests the need for an able man to fill this position.

CHAPTER X

Findings and Interpretations

Directors and Their Functions, which is part of a larger study of corporation directorates, presents the first published materials resulting from the broad analysis. Although the following findings and interpretations are mainly limited to the functioning of directors, many auxiliary questions are considered, such as: What makes a good director? What are the criticisms of directors and how can they be met? What is the significance of the controversy over "inside" and "outside" directors? Other topics, however, such as the relation of the dispersion of stock ownership to directors, the payment of directors, their tenure, the selection and election of directors, and theories about directors to represent labor, consumers, or the government are not discussed here. These and other aspects of the subject, including some of those tentatively outlined in this first publication, are being given further study and it is expected that reports on them will be published later.

Certain preliminary conclusions may be drawn from this study, but much still remains to be done before final answers can be reached. Even then it is believed that important reservations should necessarily accompany the findings. First, conclusions must be limited to the corporations studied: American industrial companies publicly owned and listed on exchanges. Second, such findings even though supported by the weight of evidence need not be final, have universal application, or be a substitute for good business judgment in specific situations. Third, they are the result of evidence of various kinds and therefore indicate standards rather than inexorable rules.

Justice Cardozo's statement about judicial reasoning applies here: "We are tending more and more toward an appreciation of the truth that, after all, there are few rules; there are chiefly standards and degrees."[1]

The approach to this study of directors and their functions has been an analysis of the practices and policies of actual companies. Four cases have been studied in detail, and brief statements are presented in Chapters IV through VII describing The American Tobacco Company, Climax Molybdenum Company, General Foods Corporation, and Standard Oil Company (New Jersey). Only by such detailed studies of various companies can the problems of directors be understood. A large number of companies have been examined in less detail. This approach has been followed not for the purpose of sanctioning present practices, but for obtaining balanced understanding from which to draw enlightening conclusions. One general and inescapable conclusion was clearly illustrated: *Directors function in many different ways and yet produce outstanding results. No standard pattern need necessarily exist.* Procedures are dictated by history, tradition, personalities, problems, products manufactured, sales methods, and industry more than by preconceived standards.

In presenting the results of this study we have not elaborated on certain fundamental premises. These concepts have been generally accepted by the directors and executives interviewed and are a part of the environment in which directors function. It is important for the sake of clarity in this conclusion to state these accepted points explicitly: (a) Although directors are elected by stockholders, they are responsible for the welfare of the entire enterprise in a very broad sense, not merely dividends for stockholders or the interests of any special group of stockholders. (b) The aim of corporate management, and the main test of its success, is profit—profit considered in the broadest sense with due regard to public interest. (c) The concept of top management includes both directors and executives.

The findings and interpretations of this study, with the limitations mentioned above, are summarized briefly under certain key questions raised by stockholders, critics, executives,

---

[1]Benjamin N. Cardozo, *The Nature of the Judicial Process* (New Haven, Yale University Press, 1921), p. 161.

and directors themselves during the various steps in this investigation.

What Are the Management Functions of a Board of Directors?

Answers to this question and the results of all investigation indicated wide variation in practice and belief.

One well-known director stated and acted on the conviction that "the only duty of a director was to secure a good president and to support him as long as he was successful." Another director furnished a long list of duties, many of which indicated his belief that he should participate in operations. Many directors acknowledged that they found their service on boards to be of great educational value. Throughout the study we encountered allegations that the main function of a director was to "get bank accounts," "get new business," or "reciprocity." Practically none of the directors interviewed, however, held these to be proper reasons for serving on a board.

In spite of the wide variations in practice, the following points are believed to outline the basic functions of an effective board of directors in discharging their responsibility for prudent management of the whole enterprise:

a. The board selects the chief executive and senior officers and makes certain that able, young executives are being developed. Also the board controls executive compensation, pension, and retirement policies.

b. The board delegates to the chief executive and his subordinate executives authority for administrative action.

c. The board discusses and approves objectives and policies of broad corporate significance, such as pricing, labor relations, expansion, and new products, as well as payment of dividends, changes in capital structure, loans, lines of credit, and public relations.

d. The board checks on the progress of the company not only as to immediate profits but also as to the discharge of its trusteeship responsibilities. Budgets, reports, inspections, and other controls aid directors in carrying out this function. They serve as the basis for the directors' most effective approach, which is to ask discerning questions from an independent outside point of view. Also, directors arrange for, control, and follow up outside audits and in general maintain vigilance for the welfare of the whole enterprise.

Referred to as frequently as were the duties of directors listed above was a popular concept as to what they should not do. "Directors should not become involved in operations except as they have official executive responsibilities....otherwise there would be confusion and disruption of executive authority."

How Are These Functions Performed?

One popular misconception about directors was that they performed their most important function by attending formal board meetings. Concurrent with this went the idea that the examination of the minutes of these formal meetings would reveal the effectiveness of the board. The author's attendance at meetings as well as his examination of minutes, however, failed completely to indicate either the chief contribution of many directors or the manner in which they performed their duties. Indeed, the assumption that regular attendance meant that directors were able and loyal at times proved misleading. Directors understood this fact better than their stockholders and the public. One director sarcastically remarked that the only function of a certain man, faithful in attendance, was to say, "I second the motion."

Although the relative importance of formal board meetings was popularly overestimated, some companies may well take more advantage of a formally convened board meeting to emphasize the importance of major decisions and to encourage critical review of performance and objectives. Furthermore, good board minutes have value in event of future misunderstandings.

Directors, however, can make contributions of great significance to a corporation by their informal activities. These contributions come through consultations with executives by telephone, at luncheon, by an exchange of letters, at committee meetings, or through visits to laboratories, factories, and offices. The responsibility of a director for corporate management involves much more than just being present at meetings; there are other, more important yardsticks of performance.

Directors may contribute much on committees. Many

directors served on executive, salary, audit, finance, and policy committees, for instance. Although there are certain weaknesses in committee work when the subjects for consideration are not carefully selected and presented or when committees usurp the functions of the board, directors can make notable contributions to corporate welfare through them.

Directors also may make real contributions by studying special as well as regular reports, thus being prepared to ask intelligent questions about proposals. In many companies executives submitted reports in advance of meetings, so that directors could study their "homework," as one director described it. Such advance reports permit them to reflect on proposals and to compare them with those in similar situations which they might have encountered in other companies.

Although the study made clear that no one pattern of organization or procedure was required for effective board action, careful planning can increase a board's effectiveness. In this planning the position of chairman is important. Efficient cooperation requires directors and executives to think through their relations in all phases of the management process. The objective is a mutual understanding in which free and critical discussion can take place on all important questions.

Have There Been Noticeable Trends in the Attitudes and Functioning of Directors?

Directors are awakening today to their responsibilities. There is a widespread concern among them to know their functions and a desire to perform them properly. Corporation directors are making exceedingly important contributions to business development, irrespective of the criticisms leveled against them and misunderstandings which have existed.

It is apparent from much testimony and evidence that in some companies the duties of directors are recognized as being vastly different from what they were considered to be in the 1920's. One director related that he had attended board meetings in that period at which the minutes were submitted for approval before any discussion had occurred. Frequently it was reported that formerly it had been considered bad taste to discuss such problems as individual executive salaries, current earnings, proposals for the purchase of companies, and other expansion plans. Executives had defended this attitude because they feared leaks of confidential information. Much of the secrecy and lack of frankness between executives and directors has been dispelled; generally questions of importance are now brought to the board for discussion.

Some important developments that have appeared are summarized as follows:

(1) During the last decade, many directors have begun to recognize more clearly their direct and implied liabilities.

(2) For the first time in the experience of many businessmen, companies find it difficult to secure able men as directors, and able men are resigning from boards. The supply is further narrowed by the policy of a number of companies, even some with outside directors themselves, which do not let their own executives serve on boards of other companies.

(3) Because of their liabilities certain directors have started to think in terms of the question, "Is this a safe step for me to approve?" rather than, "Will this help the company progress and succeed?"

(4) Directors are more concerned over what their proper responsibilities are, and some companies are defining them.

(5) They are attending meetings more regularly and devoting more time to fulfilling their responsibilities.

(6) They are considering ways of improving directorates.

(7) Salaries for directors are being advocated by some executives, directors, and others.

What Are the Characteristics of an Able Director?

Questions which arose constantly throughout the study were: Who is a good director? What makes a good director? What are the qualifications of an able director? Directors and executives were more definite in their answers to these questions than they were to the others.

There is no question but that a good director first is an able man of unquestioned personal integrity. He has courage and sound principles of business ethics. He advances and supports constructive policies for the welfare of the company regardless of conflicts with his personal interest.

Also, a good director has a background that permits him to acquire rapidly a competent grasp of the problems of the specific company in their true perspective. He has administrative skill or understands the administrative process. He has had wide experience and a broad knowledge and understanding of men and affairs. He is independent in his questions and in his judgment. He makes himself available for meetings and consultation. He is deeply interested in the success and welfare of the company in which he is a director; and he is unquestionably loyal to it. If he is proficient in any field of special interest to a specific corporation, as for example, research, the law, or labor relations, he may make especially important contributions.

Finally, able directors have a broad social point of view, an awareness of current revolutionary changes in the world, and a philosophy of their duties and responsibilities as directors.

What Is an Ideal Board of Directors?

Stockholders, directors, and executives frequently asked if the investigation revealed what the most effective board of directors might be. Those seeking the ideal, voice many criticisms of present boards, and make numerous proposals for improvements.[1] Criticisms generally fail to reach the heart of the difficulties, however. Suggested improvements frequently are superficial and create other problems.

Most proposals made in discussions over inside and outside directors, for example, disclose inadequate analysis. Certain successful and well-managed companies are criticized for having all inside executive-directors. Some stockholders and others propose that outside directors be added. It is not argued that such changes would add to the success of the company, but rather that such boards would "look better," companies would benefit from outside points of view, outside directors would eliminate what appears to be self-dealing, and outside

---

[1]Preliminary analysis was not conclusive as to the relation between board effectiveness and the number of directors on a board and their stock ownership. Some interesting statistical summaries of experience in "155 giant corporations" are shown in tables on pages 117, 122, and 123, *Business Leadership in the Large Corporation*, by Robert A. Gordon. There are some rather compelling, obvious advantages to a board near the average size of 13 directors reported by Dr. Gordon, or for boards somewhat smaller in number.

directors would be independent. Such arguments are appealing, but are not entirely reassuring when certain boards apparently so constituted were studied with care.

These discussions, however, reveal that stockholders and the public have an underlying fear of conflicts of interest, self-dealing, the failure of a board to have a critical point of view, domination of the board by the chief executive and the perpetuation of weak executives. All these faults might develop in a company with a board of outside directors. The presence of outside directors, in itself, is not enough to eliminate conflicts of personal interest and assure independence and ability, although certain boards might be improved by adding outside directors. Merely the addition of outside directors is in no sense a panacea for the ills of present-day directorates. In each case, farsighted directors should take constructive steps to clear up public misunderstanding and to remove any occasion for these criticisms.

More important to an ideal board than whether its directors are inside or outside are the integrity, ability, alertness, experience, and interest of board members. Questions of government directors, rotating directors, the number of national figures on a board, payment of directors, or attendance at board meetings are of little significance compared with the character and quality of the individuals who can be secured as directors and their personal contributions to corporate success.

The perfect board will not be found in form but rather in substance, that is, in the adaptation of the personnel and organization of a board to the specific problems of its social, political, and business environment.

How Can Boards of Directors Become More Effective?

Clarification of their trusteeship responsibilities and a better understanding of the board chairman's functions may help boards of directors to adapt themselves to their present-day problems.

The duties of top management require examination from two points of view: the administrative responsibility for getting things done, and the trusteeship responsibility for balancing all interests in corporate welfare and for avoiding personal profit at corporate expense. Both of these aspects of top management functions are not always recognized by directors and executives. This lack of clear understanding of functions and proper relationships underlies most criticisms encountered. Any board of directors which examines these two groups of responsibilities and rationally plans to discharge them both will take an important step toward increasing its effectiveness and dispelling many adverse impressions of the workings of directors and executives.

Directors need leadership to become most effective as a board in meeting their responsibility for management. To provide this leadership is the function of the board chairman, whether he is the chief executive or a separate officer. If the chief executive carries the dual responsibility for administration and for critically checking results, or if separate officers lead the board and the executive organization, the position of chairman presents a real challenge in organization and human relations. The chairman can meet the challenge through: (1) bringing before the board questions where conflicts of interest might occur, such as salary payments, pension plans, determination of dividends, review of independent audit reports, complaints of stockholders, and other problems emphasizing trusteeship; (2) supervising the selection and election of directors and executives and passing on skills and experience in management; (3) guiding attention to the policy questions emerging from executives' operating decisions; (4) proposing sound standards of board procedures; (5) drawing from directors their maximum contribution by arranging for consultation and by opening appropriate questions for board discussion and action; (6) preparing agenda that will bring regularly before the board questions and information for appropriate action.

Finally, the whole logic of the evidence needs to be reviewed: Directors and board chairmen have functions of crucial importance. These functions may be performed in almost as many different ways as there are companies. This does not mean that every board is now adequately meeting its obligations and that nothing needs to be done. Specifically, the evidence shows that improvement rests upon a thorough understanding of six major factors and their interaction in each company: (1) the present and historical composition of the stockholder group, (2) the personalities in top management, directors and executives, (3) the key problems facing the business, (4) the place of the board in the informal as well as formal organization of the company, (5) the methods of communication between the board and the executives, and (6) the extent of action by the board as a group as well as the action of directors individually.

Effective boards require adaptation to changes in social and economic trends as well as to changes in their specific companies. They cannot stop with perfunctory discharge of their formal legal responsibilities or with a narrow protective point of view. Careful diagnosis, appraisal, and treatment of each company by those interested in it are far more sound procedures than ingenious remedies prescribed wholesale.

To assume that responsibilities of directors have remained the same as they were two decades ago or that they have decreased is to ignore history and the economic development of this country. If there ever was any doubt of the importance of directors or the latent possibilities of their contributions to corporate and social welfare, it should have been dispelled by events occurring during the last decade. Directors are one of the important keys to the solution of present-day social and economic problems, and it is no exaggeration to state that national welfare, even political security and liberty, may well depend on some of their decisions concerning such matters as products, expansion, and employment.

The essential concern of corporation directors, particularly in our large corporations, is not today, nor should it ever have been, merely protection of stockholders and their interests. These functions are simply more in evidence than others. The problem is vastly more important. It is the reconciliation of private enterprise with the smooth functioning of a democratic society with justice to all groups: stockholders, executives, employees, creditors, customers, and the public. Such a broad concept of the functions of directors is frequently overlooked. Nevertheless, this should be the contribution of directors in our national life.

INDEX

INDEX

Index

Trusteeship
  definition of, 9
  responsibility of board chairman, 123-124
  responsibility of directors, 2, 5-6, 9, 14-15, 26, 30, 38, 62, 72, 102, 113, 116, 123-124, 131, 136, 137
  responsibility of top management, 14-15, 124, 127, 136
Turner et al v. The American Metal Company, Ltd., 6on

United States Steel Corporation, 121

U. S. Temporary National Economic Committee, 7n
Urwick, L., 7n

Voorhees, Enders M., 122

Weinberg, Sidney J., 71
Woodward, Ernest L., 71
Work, Bertram G., 122

Young, Owen D., 6
Young, Udell, C., 71

Zimmer, Bernard N., 57, 58

Big Business

Economic Power in a Free Society

An Arno Press Collection

La Follette, Robert Marion, editor. **The Making of America:** Industry and Finance. 1905

Lilienthal, David E. **Big Business:** A New Era. 1952

Lippincott, Isaac. **A History of Manufactures in the Ohio Valley to the Year 1860.** 1914

Lloyd, Henry Demarest. **Lords of Industry.** 1910

McConnell, Donald. **Economic Virtues in the United States.** 1930

Mellon, Andrew W. **Taxation:** The People's Business. 1924

Meyer, Balthasar Henry. **Railway Legislation in the United States.** 1909

Mills, James D. **The Art of Money Making.** 1872

Montague, Gilbert Holland. **The Rise and Progress of the Standard Oil Company.** 1904

Mosely Industrial Commission. **Reports of the Delegates of the Mosely Industrial Commission to the United States of America, Oct.-Dec., 1902.** 1903

Orth, Samuel P., compiler. **Readings on the Relation of Government to Property and Industry.** 1915

Patten, Simon N[elson]. **The Economic Basis of Protection.** 1890

Peto, Sir S[amuel] Morton. **Resources and Prospects of America.** 1866

Ripley, William Z[ebina]. **Main Street and Wall Street.** 1929

Ripley, William Z[ebina]. **Railroads:** Rates and Regulation. 1912

Rockefeller, John D. **Random Reminiscences of Men and Events.** 1909

Seager, Henry R. and Charles A. Gulick, Jr. **Trust and Corporation Problems.** 1929

Taeusch, Carl F. **Policy and Ethics in Business.** 1931

Taylor, Albion Guilford. **Labor Policies of the National Association of Manufacturers.** 1928

Vanderlip, Frank A. **Business and Education.** 1907

Van Hise, Charles R. **Concentration and Control:** A Solution of the Trust Problem in the United States. 1912

The Wealthy Citizens of New York. 1973

White, Bouck. **The Book of Daniel Drew.** 1910

Wile, Frederic William, editor. **A Century of Industrial Progress.** 1928

Wilgus, Horace L. **A Study of the United States Steel Corporation in Its Industrial and Legal Aspects.** 1901

[Youmans, Edward L., compiler] **Herbert Spencer on the Americans.** 1883

Youngman, Anna. **The Economic Causes of Great Fortunes.** 1909